THE Jack the Ripper FILES

THIS IS AN ANDRE DEUTSCH BOOK

Published in 2015 by André Deutsch Limited
An imprint of the Carlton Publishing Group
20 Mortimer Street, London W1T 3JW

Text, design and illustration copyright © André Deutsch Limited 2015

A catalogue record for this book is available from the British Library.

ISBN: 978 0 233 00473 0

Printed in Dubai

The content of this book was first published in 2008 as *Jack the
Ripper, the Casebook*.

THE

Jack the Ripper

FILES

THE ILLUSTRATED HISTORY OF
THE WHITECHAPEL MURDERS

RICHARD JONES

ANDRE
DEUTSCH

CONTENTS

INTRODUCTION

The Jack the Ripper murders took place over a ten-week period in the autumn of 1888 in London's East End. Since the killer was never caught he has left behind one of history's great whodunits and authors, researchers and the mildly curious have since dedicated themselves to solving the mystery of his identity.

But the story is interesting for many reasons. There is the almost daily reporting in the newspapers that went on throughout what has become known as "the autumn of terror". There is the opportunity the murders give us to look back at the crowded streets of the Victorian East End. There is the insight that the murders enable us to gain into the class prejudices and the social conditions of Victorian London. Then, of course, there are the mysteries that this case throws up. Who was Jack the Ripper? Where did he live? Why did he suddenly stop killing? But to hope to answer any of these questions, you need a good grounding in the case, to get to know the full sequence of events and, most importantly, to put those events into the context of the age and the streets in which they occurred.

That is what this book will do for you. You will be able to study the time line of the murders; you can read witness, police and official statements on the case. You will be able to ponder the known facts and use them to form your own conclusions. Evocative, contemporary photographs will enable you to gain an impression of what the area was like at the time of the murders. You also will be able to read case studies of the major suspects and be able to decide for yourself whether or not a particular suspect was Jack the Ripper.

In short, you have everything you need to understand and launch your own investigation into the mystery of Jack the Ripper.

LONDON IN 1888

ABOVE Life for the East End poor was a daily battle for survival.

The crimes known as the "Jack the Ripper murders" occurred in 1888, the year after Queen Victoria had celebrated her Golden Jubilee. London was then the world's largest capital city, the hub of an ever-expanding empire. The City of London, the financial boiler-room that powered that empire, had enjoyed a period of sustained economic growth, and its need for managers, clerks and administrators had seen the emergence of a new middle class that demanded, and could afford, improved living conditions.

But by 1888, things were changing. Competition from America and Germany was starting to undermine Britain's industrial pre-eminence, and a trade slump, which began the previous decade, had led to mass unemployment. Egged on by the growing socialist movement, the lower classes had begun to fight back. In 1886 and 1887, several protest rallies ended with the downtrodden masses going on the rampage in the West End of London, damaging property and looting from shops and clubs.

As a result, the middle and upper classes were beginning to worry that a revolution was inevitable, and their nervousness began to focus on the East End of London, and in particular on the district of Whitechapel. Here, a huge underclass dwelt on the periphery of the City of London and, in the opinions of many "respectable" citizens, far beyond the reach of its civilizing influence.

On the whole, the view that the middle and upper classes held about Whitechapel was largely undeserved. As Canon Samuel Barnet, the vicar of St Jude's Church on Commercial Street, and an ardent mover for social reform in the area, wrote to *The Times* at the height of the Jack the Ripper murders, "... the greater part of Whitechapel is as orderly as any part of London, and the life of most of its inhabitants is more moral than that of many whose vices are hidden by greater wealth."

But there was no denying the fact that Whitechapel had some of London's worst slums, its highest death

rates, and most dreadful living conditions. It also comprised some of the most densely populated and crime-ridden streets in the entire Victorian metropolis. Drunkenness and violence were commonplace, sexual abuse an everyday occurrence, and life itself was a daily battle for survival.

Its worst quarter was an area to the east and west of Commercial Street, where a handful of thoroughfares, such as Thrawl Street, Flower and Dean Street, and Wentworth Street, were known as the "evil quarter mile". Here, the dregs of Victorian society were crammed into slum dwellings, with as many as 20 people sharing a house and entire families living in one tiny room, sometimes supplementing the rent by subletting a corner to a lodger.

But by far the largest providers of accommodation in the "evil quarter mile" were the Common Lodging Houses, in which thousands of men, women and children slept in dormitories that, in reality, were often just rooms into which as many beds as possible had been crammed. Many of these Common Lodging Houses were well run and orderly. But a large number were

dens of iniquity, inhabited by a lawless and dangerous mix of criminals, prostitutes and the mentally unstable. Inspector Walter Dew, a local detective who began his career at Commercial Street police station in 1887, would later write in his memoirs that "even before the advent of Jack the Ripper [the district] had a reputation for vice and villainy unequalled anywhere else in the British Isles."

Although the middle and upper classes rarely, if ever, ventured into these lawless slums, they were constantly reminded of their existence. An easterly breeze might waft the overwhelming stench of sewage or the foul aroma from the area's slaughterhouses and factories into respectable nostrils. Worse still, epidemics that might begin in the slums could easily threaten bourgeois lives.

LEFT One of the busiest markets in the East End was and still is that on Petticoat Lane.

It was amid this climate of uncertainty that the famed Whitechapel Murders took place, and by conducting his reign of terror in the area that he did, and showing himself able to outwit the forces of law and order, Jack the Ripper confirmed every fear and prejudice that the middle classes had long held about the East End of London.

THE EAST END

Today the East End of London is a recognized geographic area, and is acknowledged as such the world over. But the actual term "East End" as a description of the area that lay beyond the City of London's eastern fringe was an invention of the early 1880s. However, it was quick to catch on and was embraced by the popular press, which used it to create a universal image of the area as a hotbed of villainy and degradation. As one commentator has put it, the notion of an East Ender "… became a concentrated reminder … that nothing to be found in the East End should be tolerated in a Christian country …"

THE PEOPLE OF THE ABYSS

ABOVE The port of London provided employment for a fortunate few in the area.

Of the 456,877 people who lived in the East End, a quarter of million had Whitechapel as their home, and at any one time 15,000 of its residents were classed as homeless. Disease, hunger, neglect and even violence would claim the lives of one in four children before they reached the age of five.

The populace consisted of a cross-section of Victorian society. Throughout the nineteenth century, economic migrants had been arriving in London in increasing numbers from East Anglia and Essex, both of which had seen their traditional agricultural and cloth-making industries decimated. Large numbers of Irish immigrants had also begun arriving after the potato famines of the 1840s.

Employment was intermittent. Men might find work in the docks, but this entailed turning up early at the dock gates to await the foreman, whose arrival with the sought-after employment tickets would be marked by a vicious scrum, as men kicked, punched and even bit their way to the front to ensure that they would be among the ones fortunate to earn enough money to feed their family.

Others might find work in the area's sweatshops, working in trades such as boot- and cabinet-making, or in the huge factories that dotted the district. The hours were long, the conditions were horrific, and the pay was low. Job security was non-existent, since a vast reservoir of desperate men, women and children was ever on hand to replace those unwilling to toe the line.

CHARLES BOOTH

In May 1887, Charles Booth, a wealthy shipping magnate turned philanthropist and social reporter, presented a paper to the Royal Statistical Society in which he outlined the grim reality for many who lived in the East End. Out of a population of some 456,877 people, he estimated that 22 per cent of them were living on the poverty line, while 13 per cent of them were struggling against conditions in which "decent life was not imaginable". The stark reality behind his statistics was that 60,000 East End men, women and children lived their daily lives on the brink of starvation.

BELOW The communal kitchen at a Common Lodging House. Here residents would cook their meals and socialize.

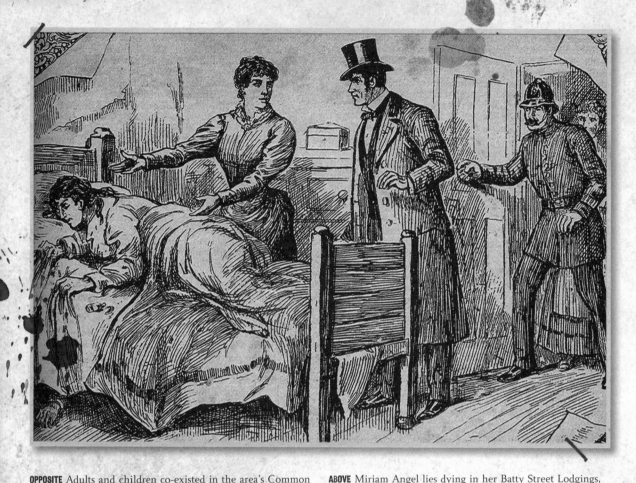

OPPOSITE Adults and children co-existed in the area's Common Lodging Houses.

ABOVE Miriam Angel lies dying in her Batty Street Lodgings, poisoned by fellow resident Israel Lipski.

By 1888, the established workforce perceived another threat to its livelihood in the form of a huge influx of Jewish immigrants who were fleeing persecution and economic hardship in Russia, Poland and Germany. Throughout the 1880s, the Jewish population of Whitechapel had increased to between 45,000 and 50,000. As the economic depression raised the spectre of mass unemployment in the area, the Jews found themselves vilified for stealing English jobs

Throughout the first part of 1888, two parliamentary committees were looking into the immigration problem. One of these was investigating the so-called Sweating system in the East End, in which employees worked in tiny, stinking workshops for anything up to 20 hours a day for minimal wages. This was seen as being particularly prevalent amongst the newly arrived Jewish immigrants. Charles Freak, Secretary of the Shoemakers' Society, a trade that was synonymous with Whitechapel, informed the committee that "These Jew foreigners work in our trade at this common work 16 or 18 hours a day and the consequence is that they make a lot of cheap and nasty stuff that destroys the market and injures us." He went on to accuse the Jewish immigrants of frustrating English workmen in their battle to attain higher wages by blacklegging during disputes and taking "work out

at any price". Another witness complained that native tradesmen were now only able to gain "a precarious living" and lamented that "Wages in tailoring, shoemaking and cabinet making, which had once stood at £2 a week, had now dropped by half to £1 and £1/5s."

The committees would ultimately vindicate the immigrants, but their prolonged deliberations ensured that the matter was in the public eye throughout the first eight months of 1888.

In June 1887, a notorious East End murder, where both the perpetrator and victim were Jewish, had shocked the area. Israel Lipski, a lodger in a house in Batty Street, had forcibly poisoned fellow lodger, Miriam Angel, by pouring nitric acid down her throat. Although he was hanged, the murder had resulted in a good deal of anti-Semitism in the area, and "Lipski" was, by 1888, being used as a term of abuse towards Jews from Gentiles.

Thus, when the Jack the Ripper murders occurred, many in the Gentile community came to the conclusion that an Englishman could not be responsible for such barbaric crimes, and they were only too willing to pin the blame on the community that they already perceived as being the cause of so many of the problems blighting their everyday lives.

UNFORTUNATES AND EVANGELISTS

It was widely perceived, and indeed was often the case, that the harshness of their living conditions dehumanized those who dwelt in the East End's slums. Childhood was all too brief, and those who survived infancy had lost all innocence by the time they reached their teens. As one commentator put it: "That people condemned to exist under such conditions take to drink and fall into sin is surely a matter for little surprise … Who can wonder that young girls wander off into a life of immorality, which promises release from such conditions?"

Women often turned to prostitution, not from any real choice, but out of economic necessity. In times of extreme hardship, many an East End family's survival came to depend on a wife or daughter prostituting herself. For the majority of middle-aged women who lived in the Common Lodging Houses – into which category all but one of Jack the Ripper's victims fell – prostitution was often the only way to earn enough

money, not only for food and lodging, but also, and often more importantly, to pay for the drink that helped them forget the nightmare of their everyday lives.

No one could be certain how many prostitutes there were in London, although General Booth, the founder of the Salvation Army, stated that the "ordinary figure

ABOVE East End women often resorted to violence to settle their differences.

LEFT A typical slum street in the East End of London.

given ... is 60,000 to 80,000". Whereas this total was probably exaggerated, including as it did those that Booth referred to as "all habitually unchaste women", it was an inescapable fact that many women from the East End slums could earn more money in one night on the streets than they could in a whole week working in a sweatshop. The allure of prostitution was obvious.

At the height of the Ripper scare the Home Office asked the police to provide statistics on the number of prostitutes in the area. Based on the observations of the constables whose beats took in the "evil quarter mile" to the east and west of Commercial Street, the police replied that they had no means of ascertaining which women were prostitutes, but that the general impression was that there were about 1,200, "mostly of a very low condition".

These low-class street prostitutes were known as "unfortunates", and night after night they would lead clients into the darkest corners of Whitechapel, to the places where they knew from experience that there was little danger of interruption. Even before Jack the Ripper began his killing spree, these women lived in constant danger: from the "bullies" (or pimps) who sought to live off them; from the gangs that would use violence to rob them of their meagre earnings; from clients wishing to avoid paying for their services; and occasionally from each other should they dare stray into another prostitute's valued territory.

Even the well-meaning activities of reformers could have an adverse affect upon them. During the winter of 1887–8, Frederick Charrington, the heir to the local brewing dynasty, had been leading a one-man crusade to rid the East End of vice. Using the terms of the Criminal Law Amendment Act of 1885, by which a citizen could report any house suspected of operating as a brothel to the police, who would then close it down,

Charrington's determined onslaught into "the foulest sinks of iniquity" had led to the closure of 200 of the area's brothels.

But his campaign had dire consequences for the displaced prostitutes. They were either forced to move to other areas – thus, as one newspaper correspondent put it, "spreading the moral contagion" – or else they had to go out and solicit on the streets in all weathers. Charrington found himself, justifiably, accused of adding to the misfortune of women who had already been "gravely wronged by men". His evangelical endeavours would be one of the reasons why so many women were forced to put their lives at risk on the streets of the East End in the autumn of 1888, since the brothels, however bad the majority might have been, would have at least have afforded them some protection from the threat of being butchered by Jack the Ripper.

ABOVE RIGHT Drinking was one of the few leisure-time activities that could be enjoyed by all.

RIGHT Frederick Charrington, whose campaign to close the East End's brothels had forced the women out onto the streets.

FREDERICK CHARRINGTON

Frederick Charrington's campaign to rid the East End of the scourge of the brothels resulted in his making a surprising discovery. Having received word that a girl was being kept against her will at a certain brothel, he took two detectives with him and went to rescue her. Having got inside and liberated the girl, they searched the rest of the house. On entering the main reception room, Charrington was astonished that his own portrait was staring down from the wall. The detectives informed him that every brothel in the area possessed a similar portrait so that the keepers would be able to recognize the man who was doing their business so much harm!

POLICING JACK THE RIPPER

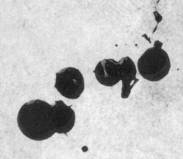

resigned, effective on 31 August 1888. The infighting between Warren and his Assistant Commissioner had left the detective department of the Metropolitan Police demoralized and in need of focused leadership to raise morale. What the department got instead was Dr Robert Anderson, a Dublin-born lawyer, who came to the post suffering from exhaustion and who, within a week of taking up office, set off for a recuperative break in Switzerland.

With Anderson away, Sir Charles Warren took command and, on 15 September 1888, informed the Home Office that if the Whitechapel Murder case was to be "successfully grappled with", it must be put into the hands of one man "who will have nothing else to concern himself with".

The officer chosen was Chief Inspector Donald Sutherland Swanson, and Warren ordered that he must

LEFT Sir Charles Warren, the Metropolitan Police Commissioner at the time of the murders.

BELOW Dr Robert Anderson was the highest-ranking officer with direct responsibility for the Jack the Ripper case.

The Whitechapel murders were investigated by two police forces, the Metropolitan Police and the City of London Police. The Metropolitan Police Commissioner was Sir Charles Warren – who, at the time of his appointment, was hailed by *The Times* as "… precisely the man whom sensible Londoners would have chosen to preside over the Police Force of the Metropolis …" But by 1888, Warren's reputation had been tarnished by his handling of what became known as "Bloody Sunday" when, on 13 November 1887, he had sent in baton-wielding police officers, soldiers and mounted police to break up a socialist demonstration in Trafalgar Square. As a result, he was very unpopular with the radical press, sections of which used the police's inability to catch Jack the Ripper as a means of exacting revenge on Warren, who found himself, unfairly in many instances, regularly maligned in the pages of several newspapers.

Warren's autocratic style of governance had also caused a conflict between him and his Assistant Commissioner in charge of the detective department, James Monro. Following almost a year of constant bickering, Monro

ABOVE Inspector Frederick George Abberline, the man who led the on-the-ground hunt for the Ripper in the area.

ABOVE Inspector Edmund Reid, one of the most respected local detectives involved in the hunt for the Whitechapel Murderer.

be given his own office and "every paper, every document, every report, every telegram must pass through his hands. He must be consulted on every subject…" Thus Swanson assumed overall charge of the case – at least until Anderson's return from holiday in early October, after which Swanson was the desk officer under him – and as the officer who assessed all the information to do with the crimes, he acquired an unrivalled knowledge of the Jack the Ripper murders.

The Metropolitan Police force was broken down into divisions, each of which had responsibility for policing a specific area of the capital. Since the Whitechapel murders, with one exception, were East End affairs, they were investigated by two divisions. The murder of Mary Nichols fell within the area policed by "J" division, while the others were investigated by "H" division. In charge of the Criminal Investigation Department of H Division was Inspector Edmund Reid, a popular detective who largely avoided the press criticism meted out to his colleagues as the quagmire of the Jack the Ripper investigation began to engulf them.

However, it was decided early on in the case to supplement these two local forces with experienced officers from the Metropolitan Police's Scotland Yard headquarters, and so Chief Inspector Moore, Inspector Abberline and Inspector Andrews were sent from Scotland Yard to head the investigation on the ground. The senior of the three officers was Inspector Abberline, and it was he who took overall charge of the investigation in the area.

One other police force investigated the Jack the Ripper crimes. The killing of Catherine Eddowes took place in Mitre Square in the City of London. Her murder, therefore, came within the jurisdiction of the City of London Police. In overall charge of the City Police was Acting Commissioner Major Henry Smith, while the head of their detective department was Inspector James McWilliam, whose principal forte was the investigation of complex financial frauds.

There were, of course, hundreds of police officers from both forces who worked to a greater or lesser extent on solving the notorious Jack the Ripper murders. But these were the ones whose names most frequently appeared during the course of the investigation.

MILE END VIGILANCE COMMITTEE

On 10 September 1888, in the wake of Annie Chapman's murder, a group of local businessmen and tradesmen got together to form the Mile End Vigilance Committee. They elected local builder Mr George Akin Lusk as their president and set about aiding the police to bring the murderer to justice. They orchestrated patrols of the area by night, and in their early days devoted their energies to raising sufficient funds to offer a reward for information. In addition, several private detectives and concerned citizens were also out on the streets by night, hoping to bring the killer to justice. Sometimes the police found it difficult to differentiate between the indigenous cranks and crackpots to whom the area was home and these self-appointed do-gooders, some of whom were themselves decidedly odd.

BELOW The press delighted in depicting the police as being helpless in their battle against crime.

THE WHITECHAPEL MURDERS BEGIN

The Jack the Ripper murders occurred in an area that comprised little more than one square mile. His victims were all prostitutes, and his crimes were seen against a wider series of killings known as the Whitechapel Murders. Since no one was ever charged, it is difficult to say with certainty how many women actually died at his hands, although historians have tended to concur with the assessment made by Sir Melville Macnaghten, Chief Constable of the Criminal Investigation Department, who in 1894 stated that Jack the Ripper had five victims. Those victims, often referred to as "the canonical five", were Mary Nichols, Annie Chapman, Elizabeth Stride, Catherine Eddowes and Mary Kelly – all of whom were murdered between 31 August and 9 November 1888. But there were in fact 11 Whitechapel Murders, two of which occurred before that of the first Ripper victim, Mary Nichols.

ABOVE It was at the junction of Osborn Street and Brick Lane in the distance that Emma Smith was attacked on 3 April 1888.

BELOW Martha Tabram spent the evening before her murder drinking in the pubs here on Whitechapel High Street.

The first Whitechapel Murder victim was Emma Smith, who, in the early hours of 3 April, was assaulted and robbed by a gang of three men on Brick Lane. She survived the initial attack, but died of peritonitis the next day. At her subsequent inquest, a verdict of "wilful murder by some person, or persons, unknown" was returned.

It is almost certain that Emma Smith was not murdered by Jack the Ripper. She was probably the victim of one of the street gangs that were known to prey on the vulnerable prostitutes of the area.

A few months later, at a little after 5 a.m. on 7 August, the body of Martha Tabram was found on the first-floor landing of a tenement building in George Yard, a dark and sinister alley located a few hundred yards from the spot where Emma Smith had been attacked. Martha had suffered a frenzied assault, and 39 stab wounds had been inflicted from her throat to her lower abdomen.

An encouraging lead was provided by Mary Anne Connelly, nicknamed "Pearly Poll", a local prostitute who later told police that she and Martha had spent the evening of 6 August drinking with two soldiers in the pubs along Whitechapel Road. Just before midnight they had split into couples and Martha had led one of the soldiers into George Yard, while Connelly took the other into the adjoining Angel Alley. Subsequent police attempts to identify the two soldiers, however, came to nothing and, once more, a verdict of murder by person or persons unknown was returned by the inquest jury.

Because her injuries were not consistent with those of the later canonical victims – she had been stabbed as opposed to ripped – Martha Tabram's murder is generally ruled out as being the work of Jack the Ripper. It should, however, be noted that her killer targeted her throat and lower abdomen, much as the Ripper would with his victims. So the possibility remains that Martha Tabram was Jack the Ripper's first victim, but that she was killed before he developed the *modus operandi* of his later crimes.

But at the time, there was little doubt that the killings were linked, and a sense of trepidation rippled through the area. The *East London Advertiser* commented that:

"… there is a feeling of insecurity to think that in a great city like London … a woman could be foully and horribly killed almost next to the citizens peacefully sleeping in their beds, without a trace or clue being left of the villain that did the deed …"

That lingering, pervasive feeling of insecurity among the population at large increased dramatically when, barely three weeks after the murder of Martha Tabram, the body of a third prostitute was discovered, this time in a dark gateway off Whitechapel Road.

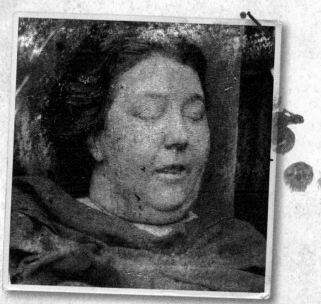

ABOVE Martha Tabram, murdered on 7 August 1888. There is debate as to whether or not she was Jack the Ripper's first victim.

BELOW Martha Tabram's body was found in a building here in George Yard at 5 a.m. on 7 August.

MURDER SCENES

In the wake of Martha Tabram's murder, several newspapers tried to convey to their readers something of the squalor of the immediate vicinity of her death. According to the *East London Advertiser*, George Yard "is a narrow turning out of the High-street, [that] leads into a number of courts and alleys in which some of the poorest of the poor, together with thieves and roughs and prostitutes, find protection and shelter in the miserable hovels bearing the name of houses." Another newspaper article described it as being "one of the most dangerous streets in the locality, and that street, together with others, has for years been a regular rendezvous and hiding place for deserters."

MARY NICHOLS

ust before 3.40 a.m. on 31 August 1888, Charles Cross, a carman (or carriageman), was heading to work along Buck's Row, a dark thoroughfare lined on one side by two-storey houses, on the other by imposing warehouses. Noticing a bundle lying in a gateway, he went to inspect it and found that it was a woman lying on the ground. Moments later, he heard footsteps behind him and turned to see another carman, Robert Paul, approaching. Calling him over, the two of them approached and crouched down over the prone form. Cross held her hands, which were quite cold. Paul leant over to see if she was breathing and as he did so his hand touched her chest and he felt it move. "I think she's breathing," he said, "but very little if she is." Paul wanted to

RIGHT P.C. Neil finds the body of Mary Nichols on 31 August 1888.

sit the woman up, but Cross refused and so the two men decided to get on their way and tell the first policeman they met of their find.

They narrowly missed Police Constable Neil who walked his beat along Buck's Row at 3.45 a.m. and shone his lantern on to the figure in the gateway. He saw blood oozing from a deep cut in her throat. Within moments he was joined at the scene by P.C. Thain whom he sent to fetch local surgeon Dr Ralph Llewellyn.

When Llewellyn arrived at a little after 4 a.m., the police officers arriving at the scene in increasing numbers were also being joined by a steady trickle of spectators from the surrounding warehouses and slaughterhouses. He carried out a cursory examination, pronounced life extinct, gave it as his opinion that, because her legs were still warm, she had not been dead more than half an hour, and then ordered the police to remove the body to the mortuary. A local resident then began washing away the congealing blood from the gateway, and soon little evidence of the murder, save a few bloodstains between the paving stones, remained.

LEFT A view looking west along Durward Street, formerly Buck's Row.

ABOVE Mary Nichols was found in the gateway on the right just before the line of cottages.

Consequently, when the senior officer, Inspector John Spratling, arrived in Buck's Row, there was nothing for him to do. He therefore hurried round to the mortuary and began taking down a description of the deceased. Lifting the woman's clothing, he made the horrific discovery that her abdomen had been ripped open.

As news of another murder spread through the district, several witnesses came forward to say that the deceased fitted the description of a woman known as Polly, who was living at a Common Lodging House in Thrawl Street. The discovery of the mark of the Lambeth Workhouse on one of the woman's petticoats led the police to Mary Ann Monk, a resident of the workhouse, who was brought to the mortuary at 7.30 p.m. and there recognized the deceased as Mary Ann Nichols. This identification enabled the police to trace her father, Edward Walker, and her estranged husband, William Nichols, both of whom confirmed her identity.

Mary Nichols, it transpired at the subsequent inquest, had been turned out of the Thrawl Street Common

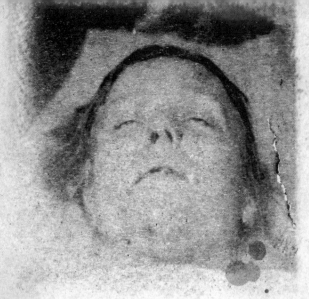

ABOVE The mortuary photograph of Mary Nichols.

Lodging House because she did not have the required four pence to pay for her bed. One of the last sightings of her was at 2.30 a.m. when her friend Ellen Holland had met her at the junction of Osborn Street and Whitechapel Road. Mary was drunk and told Ellen that she had made her doss money twice over (evidently from prostitution) but that she had spent it on drink. Ellen tried to persuade her to come back to the lodging house, but Mary refused and instead headed unsteadily off along Whitechapel Road.

At some stage in the next hour and 10 minutes, she would meet her killer and take him into the dark gateway in Buck's Row where, with ruthless and silent efficiency, he would cut her throat, slice open her abdomen and then, perhaps disturbed by the approach of Charles Cross, melt away into the night. Jack the Ripper's reign of terror had begun.

MARY NICHOLS (1845–88)

Mary Nichols was 43 years old at the time of her murder. She was 5 feet 2 inches tall, with grey eyes and greying hair. She was missing her front teeth, and a childhood accident had left a scar on her forehead. In 1864, she had married William Nichols, a printer, and the couple had five children. But by the late 1870s, Mary's drinking was becoming problematic and they separated in 1880. William kept custody of the children and provided her with an allowance of five shillings per week, but ceased paying when he learnt that she was working as a prostitute. Having viewed his wife's body at the mortuary, he emerged visibly shaken and observed "… It has come to a sad end at last."

RIGHT The memorial to Mary Nichols, the first victim of Jack the Ripper.

FAR RIGHT One of the last sightings of Mary Nichols was here at the junction of Osborn Street and Whitechapel Road.

CITY OF LONDON CEMETERY
Mary Ann Nichols
Died 31st August 1888
HERITAGE TRAIL

Metropolitan Police.

20,728 19 | 87 H. B. & Co.
1832 80,000 3 | 88 23,167

J

Division.

31st August 1888

P.C. 97 J. Neil, reports at 3.45. a.
31st inst. he found the dead body of a
woman lying on her back with her clo.
a little above her knees, with her thr.
cut from ear to ear on a yard cross.
at Bucks Row, Whitechapel, P.C.
obtained the assistance of P.C. 55 H.
Smizen and 96 J. Thain, the latter cal
Dr Llewellyn, No 152. Whitechapel Ro.
he arrived quickly and pronounce
life to be extinct, apparently but
few minutes, he directed her remo
to the Mortuary, stating he would ma
a further examination there, which
was done on the Ambulance.

Upon my arrival there and
taking a description I found that
she had been disembowelled, and at
once sent to inform the Dr of it, he
arrived quickly and on further examination stated that her throat had
been cut from left to right, two disti
cuts being on left side, the windf
gullet and spinal cord being cut
through, a bruise apparently of a the
being on right lower jaw, also one
left cheek, the abdomen had been
open from centre of bottom of ribs a
right side, under pelvis to left of the

23

Metropolitan Police.

20,296 12 | 87 H.R.&
1322 80,000 3 | 88 22.

_____ Division.

_____188

Continued

Stomach, where the wound was jag[ged]
the Omentium, or coating of the Stomach
was also cut in several places. and [the]
small stabs on private parts. apparent[ly]
done with a strong bladed knife.
Supposed to have been done by some le[ft]
handed person. death being almost in[s]-
tantous.

Description. age about 45. [len]
5 ft 2. or 3. comp[lexion] dark. hair dark [brown]
(turning grey) eyes brown. bruise on lo[wer]
right jaw and left cheek. slight l[ac]-
ation of tongue, one tooth deficien[t]
front of upper jaw; two on left of lo[wer]
do; dress. brown ulster. 7 large brass [buttons]
(figure of a female riding a horse and
man at side thereon), brown linsey f[rock]
grey woollen petticoat, flannel do, white
chest flannel, brown stays, white chem[ise]
black ribbed woollen stockings. me[n's]
S.S. boots, cut on uppers, tips on heels.
black straw bonnet, trimmed black ve[lvet]
I made enquiries and was inf[ormed]
by Mrs Emma Green, a widow, New Cot[tage]
adjoining, and Mr Walter Purkis, E[ssex]
wharf, opposite, also of William Cou[rt]
Night watchman to Messrs Brown & Ea[gle]
Bucks Row, and P.C. 81. G.E.R. Police o[n duty]
at wharf near, none of whom had [seen]

No. 6.

Metropolitan Police.

Special Report.

_____ Division.

Reference to Papers.

_____ 188

20,298 12 | 87 H. B. & Co.
1822 80,000 3 | 88 23,167

Continued

any screams during the night, or
anything to lead them to believe that
the murder had been committed there.

The Stations and Premises of the
East London and District Railways, at
the Wharves and enclosures in the
vicinity have been searched but no tr
of any weapon could be found there.

P.C. states he passed through
Row at 3.15. am. and P.S. 10. Kirby abo
the same time, but the woman wa
not there then, and is not known to the

Spratling Insp.

Keating Supt

It has since been ascertai
that the dress bears the
marks of Lambeth Work
and deceased is supposed
to have been an inmate of
that house.

Keating Supt

24

C. O. REFERENCE. | DIVISIONAL REFERENCE.

Submitted through *Executive*

Division.

Subject *Report Re Murder
of a woman unknown
at Bucks Row, White
chapel 31st inst*

31. 8. 88

12.50 pm

No. 327

*1st Special Report
submitted in accordance
with P.O. 9th Febry, 1888*

C D

*Supt.
31. 8. 88*

To A C (C & D).

D. Ct. Pearse for information

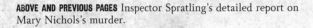

ABOVE AND PREVIOUS PAGES Inspector Spratling's detailed report on Mary Nichols's murder.

ANNIE CHAPMAN

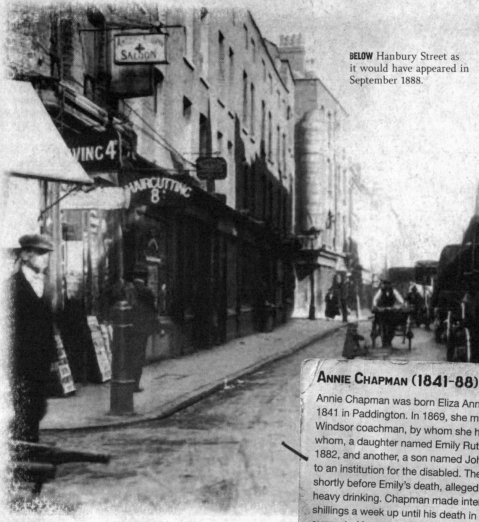

BELOW Hanbury Street as it would have appeared in September 1888.

ANNIE CHAPMAN (1841–88)

Annie Chapman was born Eliza Anne Smith in September 1841 in Paddington. In 1869, she married John Chapman, a Windsor coachman, by whom she had three children, one of whom, a daughter named Emily Ruth, died of meningitis in 1882, and another, a son named John Alfred, was confined to an institution for the disabled. The couple had separated shortly before Emily's death, allegedly as a result of Annie's heavy drinking. Chapman made intermittent payments of 10 shillings a week up until his death in 1886, and thereafter she supported herself by selling her crochet work and artificial flowers, and supplemented this income with prostitution.

In her mid 40s, Annie Chapman was short and plump, with an ashen complexion, and she was dying of consumption. A violent argument with a fellow resident at Crossingham's Lodging House in Dorset Street, where she had been living for the four months prior to her death, had left her badly bruised and suffering from a considerable amount of pain.

On the evening of 7 September, she arrived at the lodging house after several days' absence and told Timothy Donovan, its manager, that she had been in the infirmary. He allowed her to sit in the kitchen for a while, and a little after midnight sent his assistant, John Evans, to collect the money for her bed. Annie was a little the worse for drink and told him that she did not have it. She pleaded with Donovan to let her stay a little longer but, observing that she could find money

for beer but not for a bed, he ordered John Evans to escort her off the premises.

At 5.30 a.m. on 8 September, Mrs Elizabeth Long was walking along nearby Hanbury Street when she noticed a woman, whom she later identified as Annie Chapman, talking to a man outside number 29. She found nothing suspicious about their behaviour and hurried by, noting only that the man, who had his back to her, appeared to be a foreigner.

Hanbury Street was lined with four-storey houses, the rooms of which were let to individual tenants and their families. A total of 17 people lived at number 29, one of whom, John Davis, rose from his bed in the front attic room at 5.45 a.m. to get ready for work. Walking downstairs, he turned along the narrow passageway and stood on the back step. Looking down he saw a sight that sent him racing back along the passage and out into the street, where he breathlessly entreated the first three men he encountered to follow him into the house. They took one look at the dead woman and then all four of them set off to find a policeman.

The first police officer on the scene was Inspector Joseph Chandler, who was joined at 6.30 a.m. by Divisional Police Surgeon Dr George Bagster Phillips. The surgeon later surmised that the killer had grabbed Annie Chapman by the chin and partially strangled her before cutting her throat and attempting to sever her head. Her abdomen had been "entirely laid open" and the intestines had been lifted from the body and placed by the shoulder. The killer had also cut out and gone off with Annie Chapman's womb. At the inquest, Dr Phillips would propose that the removal of the womb suggested to him that the motive for her murder may have been for the killer to acquire this particular part of her anatomy. Furthermore, the speed with which the killer had removed it and the skill displayed suggested to Phillips that the murderer possessed some anatomical knowledge.

Once the body had been removed to the mortuary, the local residents discovered a surprising advantage to their sudden notoriety by charging sightseers to view the location of the murder from their windows that overlooked the site. But Annie's murder also sent a surge of terror-stricken panic through the neighbourhood, as the residents began to realize the nature of the monster loose in their midst. Mobs roamed the streets determined to wreak vengeance on anyone they thought to be responsible or involved. Innocent Jews were barracked, attacked and beaten to taunting cries that "No Englishman is capable of crimes such as these." In an attempt to contain this ugly bout of anti-Semitism, large numbers of police were drafted into the area from other parts of London. Their presence appeared to deter the killer and, for a brief period, the local populace enjoyed a respite from their autumn of terror.

BELOW At 5.30 a.m. on 8 September, Annie Chapman was seen talking to a man outside this building, 29 Hanbury Street.

BELOW Annie's body was found at 6 a.m. here in the backyard of 29 Hanbury Street.

RIGHT Annie Chapman, who is generally considered to have been the second victim of Jack the Ripper.

SUSPECTS, LUNATICS AND A LEATHER APRON

In the aftermath of the murder of Mary Nichols, police enquiries produced a promising lead when the local streetwalkers began speaking about a man whom they had nicknamed "Leather Apron". They had given him this nickname because he habitually wore such a garment, and, they said, he sometimes sported a deerstalker hat. This unsavoury character was extorting money from the prostitutes, and was not averse to beating up those who refused to give it. Local police sergeant William Thick insisted that "Leather Apron" was the nickname of a man named John, or Jack, Pizer. The police, therefore, began attempts to locate this Pizer, so that they might either establish his guilt or, if not, at least eliminate him as a suspect.

But on 5 September, *The Star* newspaper published the first of several articles that brought news of the police's suspicions to the public at large:

LEFT Chief Inspector Donald Sutherland Swanson who, in the wake of Annie Chapman's murder, was placed in overall charge of the police investigation.

BELOW The panic that followed Annie Chapman's murder led to rioting in the district, which the police struggled to contain.

> LEATHER APRON THE ONLY NAME LINKED WITH THE WHITECHAPEL MURDERS. THE STRANGE CHARACTER WHO PROWLS ABOUT AFTER MIDNIGHT. UNIVERSAL FEAR AMONG WOMEN — SLIPPERED FEET AND A SHARP LEATHER-KNIFE.

The Star went on to terrify its readers with a description of a character whose "… expression is sinister, and [who] seems to be full of terror for the women who describe it. His eyes are small and glittering. His lips are usually parted in a grin which is not only not reassuring, but excessively repellent …" According to the article, "Leather Apron" always carried a sharp knife, and it also claimed that "… he is a Jew or of Jewish parentage, his face being of a marked Hebrew type …" Determined to cause as much of a sensation as possible, the article also emphasized that "Leather Apron's" "most singular characteristic" was his ability to move noiselessly about, since the prostitutes never saw him, or even knew of his presence, until he was close by them.

The Star's articles had two consequences. Firstly, John Pizer learnt of the police's suspicions, and the prospect of his falling victim to the mob hysteria that was now surfacing in the neighbourhood so alarmed him that he decided to lie low and went into hiding among his relatives. The second effect was to cause a dramatic increase in anti-Semitism in the neighbourhood, as the articles fuelled a growing belief among the Gentile population that the crimes could not be the responsibility of an Englishman. The police and the more moderate factions of the press – some of whom even suspected that *The Star* had invented this monster – became concerned that the media sensationalism might encourage anti-Jewish riots, and attempted to dampen the speculation. But *The Star* continued its campaign. "The man is unquestionably mad," it told its readers on 6 September. "And … anybody who met him face to face would know it … his eyes are never still, but are always shifting uneasily, and he never looks anybody in the eye …"

The same article informed readers that: "The hunt for 'Leather Apron' began in earnest last evening …" and revealed that the police had begun "… a search through all the quarters where the crazy Jew was likely to be … but without result".

It was against this background that the murder of Annie Chapman occurred on 8 September, and when it was revealed that a freshly washed leather apron – which, it transpired, was unrelated to the crime or the murderer –

had been found close to the body, the anti-Semitic feeling boiled over and newspapers carried reports of riots against the Jews. As one newspaper put it: "A touch would fire the whole district in the mood in which it is now." As a consequence, policing the area became a high priority and uniformed officers were drafted in from across the metropolis in order to contain the racial unrest, as well as to instil a sense of order and security among the local populace.

On 10 September, Sergeant Thick tracked down and arrested John Pizer. But he was able to provide cast-iron alibis for the two most recent murders and was therefore ruled out as a suspect. He even appeared at Annie Chapman's inquest and was publicly cleared of any involvement in the crimes.

ABOVE Commercial Street as it looked in the autumn of 1888.

BELOW Sergeant William Thick not only investigated the murders but also found himself accused of being their perpetrator.

SERGEANT THICK

On 14 October 1889, H.T Haslewood of High Tottenham wrote to the Home Office informing them that he had received information that led him to believe that "… if Sergeant Thicke … is watched and his whereabouts ascertained upon other dates where certain women have met their end you will find the great secreate this is to be strictly private and my name is not to be mentioned." The allegation that Thick was the murderer was obviously false, and an official note in the margin dismissed it as such. But it gave Sergeant Thick the distinction of being the only one of the investigating officers to be accused on the official files of being Jack the Ripper!

JACK THE RIPPER AS A SOCIAL REFORMER

One of the more intriguing aspects of the Jack the Ripper case is the way in which social reformers latched on to the crimes as a means of publicizing to the British public the need for change in the area. By generating a huge amount of press coverage, the Ripper murders, however abhorrent, helped lay bear the grinding poverty and the awful social conditions that were the daily lot for the thousands of men, women and children who subsisted on the periphery of the City of London, the wealthiest square mile on earth.

The *Lancet* remarked that "modern society is more promptly awakened to a sense of duty by the knife of a murderer than by the pens of many earnest writers ..." In the wake of Annie Chapman's death, the *Daily Telegraph* lectured its readers on how "Dark Annie's dreadful end has compelled a hundred thousand Londoners to reflect what it must be like to have no home at all except the 'common kitchen' of a low lodging-house; to sit there, sick and weak and bruised and wretched, for lack of four pence with which to pay for the right of a 'doss'; to be turned out after midnight to earn the requisite pence, anywhere and anyhow; and in course of earning it to come across your murderer and to caress your assassin."

By the middle of September 1888, some commentators were portraying the killer as a creature spawned by the dreadful conditions of the area's slums. On 18 September in a letter to *The Times*, Sidney Godolphin Osborne warned:

ABOVE Many social commentators came to see Jack the Ripper as an inevitable outgrowth of the slums of the area.

"We have far too long been content to know that within a walk of palaces and mansions, where all that money can obtain secures whatever can contribute to make human life one of luxury ... there have existed tens of thousands of our fellow creatures begotten and reared in an atmosphere of godless brutality, a species of human sewage, the very drainage of the vilest production of ordinary vice, such sewage ever on the increase, and in its increase for ever developing fresh depths of degradation.

Just so long as the dwellings of this race continue in their present condition, their whole surroundings a sort of warren of foul alleys garnished with the flaring lamps of the gin shops, and offering to all sorts of lodgers, for all conceivable wicked purposes, every possible accommodation to further brutalize, we shall have still to go on – affecting astonishment that in such a state of things we have outbreaks from time to time of the horrors of the present day."

Godolphin's letter inspired a *Punch* cartoon which became instantly identifiable with the both the crimes and the social conditions. Titled "The Nemesis of Neglect", it depicted a shrouded, knife-wielding phantom drifting through the miasmic slums of the East End. The accompanying caption ended with admonishment, "'Tis murderous Crime – the Nemesis of Neglect!"

As the Ripper scare increased in momentum, there were calls for the closing down of the Common Lodging Houses and the wholesale redevelopment of the slums. Even Queen Victoria demanded that the dark, sinister courts and passages that riddled the area had to be lit at night. On 24 September, George Bernard Shaw wrote to *The Star* to theorize about the killer's motive:

> "SIR,-- Will you allow me to make a comment on the success of the Whitechapel murderer in calling attention for a moment to the social question? … Private enterprise has succeeded where Socialism failed. Whilst we conventional Social Democrats were wasting our time on education, agitation, and organisation, some independent genius has taken the matter in hand, and by simply murdering and disembowelling four women, converted the proprietary press to an inept sort of communism."

Obviously, Shaw was being ironic when he applauded the killer's success as a social reformer, but what cannot be denied is that the Whitechapel Murders most certainly drew attention to the dreadful living conditions in the area, and several of the improvements, although bound to happen eventually, were speeded up thanks to the increased attention that the killings had focused on the neighbourhood.

ABOVE George Bernard Shaw was one of the first to suggest that Jack the Ripper may have been a social reformer.

RIGHT Even Queen Victoria felt moved to comment on conditions in the area and demanded that all the dark courtyards be lit by night.

ROYAL INTERVENTION

In the wake of Mary Kelly's murder, even Queen Victoria made her concerns known about the conditions in the area and the abilities of the police force. She sent an angry missive to her Prime Minister, Lord Salisbury, in which she railed: "This new most ghastly murder shows the absolute necessity for some very decided action. All these courts must be lit, & our detectives improved. They are not what they should be." One wonders how the Queen would have reacted had she known that, in about 100 years, the theory that the killer had been a member of her own family would be receiving a wide circulation!

ELIZABETH STRIDE

lisabeth Gustafsdotter was born in Torslanda, Sweden, in 1843. She moved to London in 1866, and three years later married John Thomas Stride and changed her name to Elizabeth Stride. The couple separated in around 1877, and Elizabeth, or "Long Liz" as she was nicknamed, began the familiar downward spiral into the drink-fuelled, prostitution-funded lifestyle of all Jack the Ripper's victims.

By 1888, Elizabeth Stride was staying, off and on, at a Common Lodging House at 32 Flower and Dean Street, where she spent the afternoon of 29 September cleaning two rooms. The deputy keeper, Elizabeth Tanner, paid her sixpence for this, and by 6.30 p.m. Stride was enjoying a drink in the nearby Queen's Head pub. Having returned to the lodging house, she smartened herself up and cheerfully bade fellow residents goodbye.

It rained that night and at 11 p.m. she was seen sheltering with a man in the doorway of the Bricklayers' Arms Pub on Settle Street by two labourers, J. Best and John Gardner. They told the inquest that they were surprised at how the man was hugging and kissing her. Prophetically the two men jested, "Watch out, that's Leather Apron getting around you!" Embarrassed, the couple hurried off.

Elizabeth Stride then made her way over to nearby Berner Street, where several witnesses claimed to have seen her over the next hour in the company of a man.

ABOVE Several witnesses reported sightings of Elizabeth Stride in the hours before her murder.

BELOW The murder of Elizabeth Stride took place here in Berner Street.

These included P.C. William Smith who at 12.30 a.m. saw a man and a woman, whom he later identified as Stride, standing in the gateway of Dutfield's Yard, a dark and narrow court that led off Berner Street.

At around 12.45 a.m., Israel Schwartz was heading home along Berner Street when he saw a man attack a woman in the gateway to Dutfield's Yard. Unwilling to get involved, Schwartz crossed over the road and noticed a man smoking a pipe in the doorway of a beer shop. At this point, the man attacking the woman looked up and shouted "Lipski!" in the direction of him and the other man. According to Schwartz, the man in the doorway then began to follow him and, fearing for his own safety, Schwartz ran off. Since it is likely that Schwartz witnessed the early stages of Stride's murder, the presence of the second man has suggested to some that the Ripper had an accomplice. However, it appears that the police managed to trace this mystery figure and that he was ruled out of being involved in the killing.

At 1 a.m. Louis Diemshutz, the steward of the Jewish Socialist Club that overlooked Dutfield's Yard, arrived back from a day spent hawking cheap jewellery at Westerhill

Dr Barnardo

Dr Thomas Barnardo, who at the time was campaigning to have it made illegal for young children to be admitted to Common Lodging Houses, later recalled that he had visited 32 Flower and Dean Street to solicit the views of the women who lived there on the issue. He told them of his scheme to save children from what he called the "contamination of the Common Lodging Houses" and all of them were very supportive of the idea. Visiting the mortuary in the wake of Elizabeth Stride's murder, he immediately recognized her as one of the women he had spoken with.

Market, Crystal Palace. As he turned his pony and cart into the yard, the pony shied left and stood still. Looking into the darkness, Diemshutz saw a bundle on the ground and tried to lift it with his whip. Unable to do so, he jumped down, struck a match and found a woman lying on the ground. Hurrying into the club he fetched a candle and, with several members, returned to the yard. They saw that the woman's throat had been severed by what Diemshutz would later describe as "a great gash two inches wide".

But it transpired that the rest of the body had not been mutilated, which led the police to surmise that the killer had been interrupted, probably by Diemshutz. As he made his initial find, the murderer may well have still been in the yard, standing alongside him in the darkness. The few minutes during which Diemshutz went to raise the alarm gave the murderer his opportunity to hurry from Berner Street and make his way into the City of London where, in another dark corner, he claimed his next victim.

ABOVE LEFT The mortuary photograph of Jack the Ripper victim Elizabeth Stride.

LEFT The murderer may well have been interrupted as he murdered Elizabeth Stride and only just managed to escape.

METROPOLITAN POLICE.

CRIMINAL INVESTIGATION DEPARTMENT,
SCOTLAND YARD,

19th day of October 1888

SUBJECT Murder of
Elizabeth Stride at Duf-
fields yard Berner St.
Body found at 1 am
30th Sept 1888.

REFERENCE TO PAPERS.

I beg to report that the following are
the particulars respecting the murder of
Elizabeth Stride on the morning of
30th Sept. 1888. ——

1am. 30th Sept.   A body of a woman was found
with the throat cut, but not
otherwise mutilated by Louis
Diemshitz (Secretary to the
Socialist Club) inside the gates
of Duffield's Yard in Berner St.
Commercial Road East. who
gave information to the police.
P.C 252 Lamb proceeded with
them to the spot & sent for
Drs Blackwell & Phillips.

1.10 am.   Body examined by the Doctors
mentioned who pronounced
life extinct, the position of
the body was as follows:—
lying on left side, left arm
extended from elbow, cachous
lying in hand, right arm over
stomach back of hand & inner
surface of wrist dotted with
blood

23,939 7 | 88 H. B. & Cc.
506 2000 7 | 88 25,939

blood, legs drawn up Knees fixed feet close to wall, body still warm silk handkerchief round throat, slightly torn corresponding to the angle of right jaw, throat deeply gashed and below the right angle apparent abrasion of skin about an inch and a quarter in diameter.

Search was made in the yard but no instrument found.

From enquiries made it was found that at :———

12.35am 30ᵗ P.C. 452ᴴ Smith saw a man and woman the latter with a red rose talking in Berner Street this P.C. on seeing the body identified it as being that of the woman whom he had seen & he thus describes the man as age about 28. ht 5 ft. 7 in: comp. dark, small dark moustache, dress black diagonal coat, hard felt hat, white collar & tie.

12.45am 30ᵗ Israel Schwartz of 22 Helen Street

Street, Backchurch Lane stated, that at that hour on turning into Berner St. from Commercial Road & had got as far as the gateway where the murder was committed he saw a man stop & speak to a woman, who was standing in the gateway. The man tried to pull the woman into the street, but he turned her round & threw her down on the footway & the woman screamed three times, but not very loudly. On crossing to the opposite side of the street, he saw a second man standing lighting his pipe. The man who threw the woman down called out apparently to the man on the opposite side of the road "Lipski" & then Schwartz walked away, but finding that he was followed by the second man he ran as far as the railway arch but the man did not follow so far.

The use of "Lipski" increases my belief that the murderer was a Jew

36

Schwartz cannot say whether
the two men were together
or known to each other.
Upon being taken to the
Mortuary Schwartz identified
the body as that of the woman
he had seen & he thus describes
the first man who threw the
woman down :- age about
30 ht. 5ft. 5in comp. fair
hair dark, small brown moustache
full face, broad shouldered.
dress, dark jacket & trousers
black cap with peak, had nothing
in his hands.

second man age 35 ht. 5ft. 11in
comp. fresh, hair light brown,
moustache brown, dress dark
overcoat, old black hard felt
hat wide brim, had a clay
pipe in his hand

about 1 am 30th Leon Goldstein of 22 Christian
Street Commercial Road, called
at Leman St. & stated that he
was the man that passed down
Berner St. with a black bag at
that

that hour, that the bag
contained empty cigarette
boxes & that he had left a
coffee house in Spectacle Alley
a short time before.

The description of the man seen by the P.C.
was circulated amongst police by wire, &
by authority of Commissioner it was
also given to the press. On the evening
of 30th the man Schwartz gave the
description of the men he had seen ten
minutes later than the P.C. and it was
circulated by wire. It will be observed
that allowing for differences of opinion
between the P.C. & Schwartz as to apparent
age & height of the man each saw with
the woman whose body they both identified there are serious differences in the
description of dress :- thus the P.C. describes
the dress of the man whom he saw as
black diagonal coat, hard felt hat, while
Schwartz describes the dress of the man he
saw as dark jacket black cap with peak.
so that at least it is rendered doubtful
whether they are describing the same man
If Schwartz is to be believed, and
the

Who saw this man go down Berners St.? or did he come forward to clear himself in case any questions might be asked

the police report of his statement casts
no doubt upon it, it follows if they
are describing different men that the
man Schwartz saw & described is the
more probable of the two to be the
murderer, for a quarter of an hour
afterwards the body is found murdered.
At the same time account must be taken
of the fact that the throat only of the
victim was cut in this instance which
measured by time, considering meeting
(if with a man other than Schwartz saw)
the time for the agreement & the murderous
action would I think be a question of
so many minutes, five at least, ten at
most, so that I respectfully submit it
is not clearly proved that the man that
Schwartz saw is the murderer although
it is clearly the more probable of the two.
Before concluding in dealing with the
descriptions of these two men I venture
to insert here for the purpose of compar
ison with these two descriptions, the
description of a man seen with a woman
in Church Passage close to Mitre Square
at 1.35 a.m. 30th by two men coming
out

This is rather confused: at 12.30
If the man whom the P.C. saw is not
the same as the man whom
Schwartz saw, at 12.45 then it is clearly
more probable that the man whom
Schwartz saw was the murderer,
because Schwartz saw his man
a quarter of an hour later than
the P.C.
But I understand the Inspector to
suggest that Schwartz' man need
not have been the murderer
For only 15 minutes elapsed
between 12.45 when Schwartz
saw the man & 1.0 when
the woman was found murdered
on the same spot. But the
suggestion is that Schwartz' man
may have left her, she being
a prostitute the assault or
was assaulted by another man,
& there was time enough for
this to take place & for this
other man to murder her
before 1.0

The Police apparently do not suspect
the 2nd man whom Schwartz saw
on the other side of the street
& who followed Schwartz

out of a club close by :— age 30 ht 5 ft
7 or 8 in. comp fair, fair moustache
medium build, dress pepper & salt color
loose jacket, grey cloth cap with peak of
same color, reddish handkerchief tied
in a knot. round neck, appearance of
a sailor. In this case I understand
from the City Police that Mr Lewin
one of the men identified the clothes
only of the murdered woman Eddowes.
which is a serious drawback to the
value of the description of the man
Ten minutes afterwards the body is
found horribly mutilated & it is therefore
reasonable to believe that the man he
saw was the murderer, but for_{^purposes of} com-
-parison, this description is nearer to
that given by Schwartz than to that
given by the P.C.

The body was identified as that of
Elizabeth Stride, a prostitute, & it may
be shortly stated that the enquiry
into her history did not disclose the
slightest pretext for a motive on behalf
of friends or associates or anybody who
had known her. The action of Police
                                    besides

The woman murdered
in the City

besides being continued in the directions
mentioned in the report respecting the
murder of Annie Chapman was as
follows

a. Immediately after the police were
on the spot the whole of the members
who were in the Socialist Club
were searched, their clothes examined
and their statements taken.

b Extended enquiries were made in
Berner Street to ascertain if any
person was seen with the woman

c Leaflets were printed & distributed
in H Division asking the occupiers
of houses to give information to
Police of any suspicious persons
lodging in their houses.

d The numerous statements made to
Police were enquired into and the
Persons (of whom there were many)
were required to account for their
presence at the time of the murders
& every care taken as far as possible
to verify the statements.

Concurrently with enquiry under head
a the yard where the body was found
was

was searched but no instrument was
found.

Arising out of heading b, a, Mr
Packer a fruiterer, of Berner St. stated
that at 11 p.m. 29th Sept. a young man
age 25 to 30 about 5 ft. 7 in. dress long
black coat, buttoned up, soft felt hat,
(kind of Yankee hat) rather broad shoulders,
rough voice, rather quick speaking,
with a woman wearing a geranium
like flower, white outside, red inside,
& he sold him 1/2 lb of grapes. The man
& woman went to the other side of road
& stood talking till 11.30 p.m. then they
went towards the Club (Socialist)
apparently listening to the music. Mr
Packer when asked by the Police stated
that he did not see any suspicious person
about, and it was not until after the
publication in the newspapers of the
description of man seen by the P.C.
that Mr Packer gave the foregoing particulars to two private enquiry men
acting conjointly with the Vigilance
Comtee and the Press, who upon searching a drain in the yard found a grape
stem

stem which was amongst the other
matter swept from the yard after its
examination by the police & then calling
upon Mr Packer whom they took to the
mortuary where he identified the body
of Elizabeth Stride as that of the woman.
Packer who is an elderly man, has
unfortunately made different statements
so that apart from the fact of the
hour at which he saw the woman
(and she was seen afterwards by the
P.C. & Schwartz as stated) any statement
he made would be rendered almost
valueless as evidence,

Under head C. 80,000 pamphlets
to occupier were issued and a house
to house enquiry made not only involving the result of enquiries from the
occupiers but also a search by Police
& with a few exceptions - but not such
as to convey suspicion - covered the area
bounded by the City Police boundary
on the one hand, Lamb St. Commercial
St. Great Eastern Railway & Buxton St.
then by Albert St. Dunk St. Chicksand
St. & Great Garden St to Whitechapel Rd
and

then to the City boundary, under this head also Common Lodging Houses were visited & over 2000 lodgers were examined.

Enquiry was also made by Thames Police as to sailors on board ships in Docks or river & extended enquiry as to Asiatics present in London, about 80 persons have been detained at the different Police Stations in the Metro--polis & their statements taken and verified by police & enquiry has been made into the movements of a number of persons estimated at upwards of 300 respecting whom communications were received by police & such enquiries are being continued.

Seventy six Butchers & Slaughterers have been visited & the characters of the men employed enquired into, this embraces all servants who had been employed for the past six months.

Enquiries have also been made as to the alleged presence in London of Greek Gipsies, but it was found that they had not been in London during

during the times of the various murders

Three of the persons calling
themselves Cowboys who belonged to
the American Exhibition were traced
& satisfactorily accounted for themselves.

Up to date although the
number of letters daily is considerably
lessened, the other enquiries respecting
alleged suspicious persons continues as
numerous

There are now 994 Dockets
besides police reports.

     (sd) Donald S. Swanson
      Ch: Inspt.

CATHERINE EDDOWES

At 8.30 p.m. on 29 September Catherine Eddowes had been arrested for causing a drunken disturbance on Aldgate High Street. She was taken to Bishopsgate Police Station and locked in a cell, where she promptly fell asleep. Sobering up around midnight, she awoke and was released at 12.55 a.m. As she left the police station, the duty officer, P.C. Hutt, told her to close the door behind her. "All right," was Catherine's chirpy reply. "Good night Old Cock." So saying, she turned left and walked off in the direction of Houndsditch. Hutt later estimated that it would have taken about eight minutes for her to reach Mitre Square.

Mitre Square, situated just inside the City of London's eastern boundary, was an enclosed square over which towered imposing warehouse buildings. Three uninhabited houses and a shop backed onto its south-west corner. Two further houses, one of which was occupied by a City policeman, huddled between the warehouses. The square had three entrances: a fairly wide one that led from Mitre Street; the narrower St James's Passage in its north-east corner; and the long, narrow Church Passage that led from its south-east corner and out on to Duke Street.

At 1.30 a.m., P.C. Watkins of the City Police passed this south-east corner and found the square to be deserted and quiet. Five minutes later, Harry Harris, Joseph Levy and Joseph Lawende left the Imperial Club on Duke Street and passed a man and woman who were talking quietly at the junction of Duke Street and Church Passage. Although the woman had her back to them, Joseph Lawende was later certain that it had been Catherine Eddowes, albeit he made his identification from her clothing, which he was shown at the police station. Lawende did see the man's face and described him as having the appearance of a sailor. He was aged about 30; around 5 feet 9 inches (175 centimetres) tall; of medium build with a fair complexion and a small, fair moustache. But since the couple were just chatting, he paid them little attention and was later adamant that he would not recognize nor be able to identify the man should he see him again.

ABOVE, TOP Catherine Eddowes was arrested for being drunk here on Aldgate High Street the evening before her murder.

ABOVE Around midnight Catherine Eddowes had sobered up and was heard singing in her cell at Bishopsgate Police Station.

LEFT Her body was found in Mitre Square 45 minutes after she had been released.

ABOVE Police Constable Watkins raises the alarm after finding the body of Catherine Eddowes.

At 1.44 a.m., P.C. Watkins returned to Mitre Square and found Catherine's body lying in a pool of blood in the dark south-west corner. She had suffered a frenzied and horrendous attack. Her throat had been cut, almost back to the spine. Her abdomen had been ripped open and savagely mutilated. V-shaped incisions that pointed upwards towards her eyes had been carved into her cheeks. Her eyelids had been nicked through, as had her earlobes. The tip of her nose had been sliced off and half her uterus and her left kidney had been taken away, along with a portion of the apron she was wearing.

Watkins quickly raised the alarm, and policemen were soon converging on Mitre Square from all directions. Yet once again the killer had simply melted away. George Morris, a retired police officer who was working as a night watchman in the warehouse opposite the murder spot – and who had been the first person alerted by P.C. Watkins after he found the body – later expressed his bafflement as to how the murder could have been committed so close to him without his hearing anything.

According to the *Illustrated Police News*, Morris "… could hear the footsteps of the policeman as he passed on his beat every quarter of an hour, so that it appeared impossible that the woman could have uttered any sound without his detecting it. It was only on the night that he remarked to some policeman that he wished the 'butcher' would come round Mitre Square and he would give him a doing; yet the 'butcher' had come and he was perfectly ignorant of it …"

Determined that the perpetrator would not evade them, the City Police were soon fanning out into the surrounding streets. Then, a little over an hour later, word arrived that the missing portion of apron had been found in a nearby doorway. The City detectives hurried to investigate, only to find themselves at loggerheads with their colleagues in the Metropolitan Police.

RIGHT The horrific injuries suffered by Catherine Eddowes are clearly visible in this mortuary photograph of her body.

BELOW Her murderer had mutilated Catherine Eddowes's face.

CATHERINE EDDOWES (1842-88)

Catherine Eddowes was born in Wolverhampton. In her early twenties she had taken up with army pensioner Thomas Conway, whom she claimed she had married. They had three children, but separated in 1880 due to Catherine's habitual drinking. She then became involved with Irish porter John Kelly and they stayed together until the time of her death. In September 1888, the couple went hop-picking in Kent, but having failed to make a great deal of money, returned to London and spent the night of 27 September at the Shoe Lane casual ward. Here, she reputedly told the superintendent that she had come back to claim the reward being offered for the capture of the Whitechapel Murderer. He told her to be careful that she didn't end up murdered herself, to which she allegedly replied, "Oh, no fear of that."

METROPOLITAN POLICE.

CENTRAL OFFICER'S } SPECIAL REPORT. }

SUBJECT Jack known to Met. Police respecting the Murder in Mitre Square & writing on wall.

REFERENCE TO PAPERS.

CRIMINAL INVESTIGATION DEPARTMENT,
SCOTLAND YARD,

6th day of November 188 8

I beg to report that the facts concerning the murder in Mitre Square which came to the knowledge of the Metropolitan Police are as follows:—

1.45 a.m. 30th Sept. Police Constable Watkins of the City Police discovered in Mitre Square the body of a woman, with her face mutilated almost beyond identity, portion of the nose being cut off; the lobe of the right ear nearly severed. the face cut; the throat cut. and disembowelled. The P.C. called to his assistance Mr Morris, a night watch and pensioner from Metrop police. from premises looking on the Square. and surgical aid was subsequently called in. short details of which will be given further on in this report.

The City police having been made acquainted with the facts by P.C. Watkins the following are the results of their Enquiries so far as known to Met. Police:—

1.30 a.m. The P.C. passed the spot where the body was found at 1.45 a.m. and there was nothing to be seen there at that time.

1.35 a.m. Three Jews, one of whom is named Mr Levin. left a Club, in Duke Street; and Mr Lawende saw a man talking to a woman in Church Passage which leads directly to Mitre Square. The other two took but little notice and state that they could not identify a man or woman. and even Mr Lawende states that he could not identify the man; but as the woman stood with her back to him. with her head on the man's breast. he could not identify the body mutilated

---

THIS AND FOLLOWING PAGES Chief Inspector Swanson's report on the Mitre Square murder of Catherine Eddowes.

mutilated as it was, as that
of the woman whose back he
had seen. but to the best of
his belief the clothing of the
deceased, which was black
was similar to that worn by
the woman whom he had seen
and that was the full extent
of his identity,-

2. 20 am. P.C. 254ᵃ Long (the P.C. was
    drafted from A Division temporarily
    to assist "H" Division) stated that
    at the hour mentioned he
    visited Goldston Street Buildings
    and there was nothing there at
    that time. but at:-

2. 55 am. he found in the bottom
    of a common stairs leading
    to Nᵒ 108 & 119. Goldston Street
    Buildings a piece of a
    bloodstained apron. and
    above it written in chalk. the
    words. "The Juwes are the men
    who will not be blamed for
    nothing". which he reported.
    and the City Police were

subsequently

acquainted at the earliest
moment; when it was formed
that beyond doubt. the piece
of apron formed corresponded
exactly with the part missing
from the body of the murdered
woman.

The Surgeon, Dᵣ Brown called by the
City Police, and Dᵣ Phillips who had
been called by the Metropolitan
Police in the cases of Hanbury Street
and Berner st; having made a
post mortem examination of the
body reported that there were
missing the left kidney and the
uterus, and that the mutilation so
far gave no evidence of anatomical
knowledge in the sense that it
evidenced the hand of a qualified
surgeon, so that the Police could
narrow their enquiries into certain
classes of persons. On the other
hand as in the Metropolitan Police
cases, the medical evidence shewed
that the murder could have been
committed by a person who had

been

been a hunter, a butcher, a slaughter-
man, as well as a student in surgery
or a properly qualified surgeon.

The result of the City Police
enquiries were as follow: - beside
the body were found some pawn-
-tickets in a tin box, but upon
tracing them, they were found to
relate to pledges made by the
deceased, who was separated
from her husband, and was living
in adultery with a man named
John Kelly, respecting whom Enquiry was at once made by Metropolitan and City Police, the result
of which was to shew clearly that
he was not the murderer. Further
it shewed that the deceased's
name was Catherine Eddowes, or
Conway, who had been locked
up for drunkenness at Bishopsgate Street Police Station at 8.45
P.m. 29th and, being sober was discharged at 1 A.m. 30th. Enquiry
was also made by the City and
Metropolitan

Metropolitan Police conjointly
into her antecedents, and it was
found that there did not exist
amongst her relations or friends
the slightest pretext for a motive
to commit the murder.
At the Goldston Street Buildings
where the portion of the blood-stained
apron was found the City Police
made Enquiry, but unsuccessfully,
and their subsequent Enquiries
into matters affecting persons
suspected by correspondence, or
by statements of individuals at
Police Stations, as yet without
success, have been carried on
with the knowledge of the Metropolitan
Police, who on the other hand
have daily acquainted the City
Police with the subjects and
natures of their enquiries.
Upon the discovery of the
blurred chalk writing on the
wall, written - although mis-spelled
in the second word. - in an ordinary
hand in the midst of a locality
principally

principally inhabited by Jews of all nationalities as well as English, and upon the wall of a common stair leading to a number of tenements occupied almost exclusively by Jews, and the purport of the writing as shewn at page 3. was to throw blame upon the Jews; the Comm' deemed it advisable to have them rubbed out. Apart from this there was the fact that during police enquiries into the Bucks Row and Hanbury Street murders, a certain section of the Press cast a great amount of suspicion upon a Jew, named John Pizer, alias "Leather Apron" as having been the murderer whose movements at the dates and hours of those murders had been satisfactorily enquired into by Met: Police, clearing him of any connection, there was also the fact that on the same morning another murder had been

been committed in the immediate vicinity of a Socialist Club in Berner Street. frequented by Jews. – Considerations, which, weighed in the balance, with the evidence of chalk writing on the wall to bring home guilt to any person, were deemed the weightier of the two. To those police officers who saw the chalk writing, the handwriting of the now notorious letters to a newspaper agency bears no resemblance at all.

Rewards were offered by the City Police and by Mr Montagu and a Vigilance Committee formed presided over by Mr Lusk of Alderney Road, Mile End, and it is to be regretted that the combined result has been. that no information leading to the murderer has been forthcoming. On the 18th Oct. Mr Lusk brought a parcel. which had been addressed to him to Leman Street. The parcel contained what

51

192

what appeared to be a portion of a Kidney. He received it on 15th Oct. and submitted it for examination eventually to Dr. Openshaw. Curator of London Hospital Museum who pronounced it to be a human Kidney. The Kidney was at once handed over to the City Police, and the result of the combined medical opinion they have taken upon it, is, that it is the Kidney of a human adult; not charged with a fluid, as it would have been in the case of a body handed over for purposes of dissection to an hospital, but rather as it would be in a case where it was taken from the body not so destined. In other words similar kidneys might & could be obtained from any dead person upon whom a post mortem had been made from any cause by students or dissecting room porters. The Kidney, or rather portion of the Kidney, was accompanied by a letter couched as follows.—

as the any such mort. made within a week in the E. or E.C. districts.

193

From hell.

Mr Lusk
Sor
I send you half the Kidne I took from one women prasarved it for you. tother piece I fried and ate it was very nise. I may send you the bloody knif that took it out if you only wate a whil longer
signed Catch me when you can
Mishter Lusk.

The postmarks upon the parcel are so indistinct that it cannot be said whether the parcel was posted in the E. or E.C. districts; and there is no envelope to the letter. and the City Police are therefore unable to prosecute any enquiries upon it.

The remaining Enquiries of the City Police are merged into those of the Metropolitan Police, each Force cordially

Communicati[ng]

Communicating to the other daily
the nature and subject of their
Enquiries.

The foregoing are the facts so
far as known to Metropolitan
Police, relating to the murder in
Mitre Square.

Donald S. Swanson.
Ch. Inspector.

Copy of
REPORT
Div.
Detective
Department

163

29 OCT.88

CITY OF LONDON POLICE.

October 27th 1888

Re East End Murders.

I beg to report with reference to the recent murders in Whitechapel that, acting upon stringent orders issued by the Commissioner with a view to prevent if possible a repetition of the murders which had previously been committed in Whitechapel and to keep a close observation upon all Prostitutes frequenting public houses and walking the Streets, extra men in plain clothes have been employed by this department since August last to patrol the Eastern portion of the City. On the 30th September at 1.45 a.m. a woman since identified as Catherine Eddowes was found with her throat cut & disembowelled in Mitre Square Aldgate about 300 yards from the City boundary. The Constable who found the body immediately sent for a Surgeon and also to the Police Station at Bishopsgate Street and Inspector Collard was on the spot in a few minutes. Detective

164

Detective Constables Halse, Marriott & Outram who had been searching the passages of houses in the immediate neighbourhood of the spot where the murder was committed (& where the doors are left open all night) on hearing of the murder at 1.55 a.m. at once started off in various directions to look for suspected persons. The Officer Halse also went in the direction of Whitechapel and passed through Goulstone Street — where part of the deceased's apron was subsequently found at 2.30 a.m.; on returning to the Square he heard that part of an apron stained with blood had been found in Goulstone Street, he then went with D.S. Lawley & D.C. Hunt to Leman Street Station & from thence to Goulstone Street where the spot at which the apron was found was pointed out to him. On the wall above it was written in chalk "The Jewes are the men that "will not be blamed for nothing". Halse remained by the writing and Lawley and Hunt returned to Mitre Square.

(2)

THIS AND FOLLOWING PAGES Inspector McWilliam's report on the police response to Catherine Eddowe's murder as well as the related issues of the graffito and anonymous letter.

54

165

In the meantime I had been
informed of the murder and arrived
at the Detective Office at 3.45 a.m,
after ascertaining from S.S. Izzard
what steps he had taken in consequence
of it; I wired to Scotland Yard
informing the Metropolitan Police of
the murder and went with D.S. Dowens
to Bishopsgate Station & from thence
to Mitre Square. I there found
Major Smith, Superintendent Foster,
Inspector Collard & several Detective
Officers. Hawley & Aunt informed
me of the finding of the apron &
the wording on the wall, the latter of
which I ordered to be photographed
and directed the Officers to return
at once & search the "Model"
dwellings & lodging houses in the
neighbourhood. I then went to
the Mortuary in Golden Lane, where
the body had been taken by direct
of Dr Gordon-Brown and saw
piece of apron—which was found
Goulstone Street—compared with a
piece the deceased was wearing
it exactly corresponded. I then return
to the Detective Office and had

(3)

166

had telegraphed to the Divisions and
Metropolitan Police a description of the
murdered woman and her clothing.
Additional officers had then arrived
and they were sent out in various
directions to make Enquiry. On Monday
the 1st October on the recommendation of
the Commissioner, the Lord Mayor
authorised a reward of £500 to be
offered. Printed bills were at once
ordered & circulated, in response to
which a great many communications
have been received & are still coming
in. Enquiry was also made with a
view to get the deceased identified
and on the 3rd Inst it was ascertained
that her name was Catherine Eddowes
& that she had been living with a man
named Kelly at Cooney's lodging house
Flower and Dean Street, Spitalfields
She had lived with Kelly for seven or
Eight years, prior to which she had lived
with a man named Thomas Conway
a pensioner for about twenty years
& had three children by him—two
sons & a daughter, but Conway was
Eventually compelled to leave her
on account of her drunken and

(4)

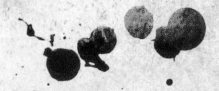

and immoral habits. Considerable difficulty was experienced in finding Conway in consequence of his having enlisted in the name of Thomas Quinn, he was found however, also the three children & two sisters of the deceased.

On Thursday the 4th Inst, an Inquest was held at the Mortuary by S. F. Langham Esq "Coroner" & a Jury and adjourned till the 11th Instant, when a Verdict of "Wilful Murder against some person unknown" was returned. Every Effort has been made to trace the murderer, but up to the present without success. Enquiry has been made respecting persons in almost every Class of Society & I have sent officers to all the Lunatic Asylums in London to make Enquiry respecting persons recently admitted or discharged: many persons being of opinion that these crimes are of too revolting a character to have been committed by a sane person.

The Enquiry is still being actively followed up, but the Police are at a great disadvantage in this Case

(5)

in consequence of the want of identity. No one having seen the deceased from the time she was discharged from Bishopsgate Station until her body was found at 1.45 a.m, except three gentlemen who were leaving the Imperial Club in Duke Street at 1.35 a.m, and who state that to the best of their belief they saw her with a man in Church Passage at that time, but took no particular notice of them. One of the gentlemen Mr. Lawende of 79 Fenchurch Street who was nearest to the man & woman & saw most of them, says he does not think he should know the man again, and he did not see the woman's face. No other person can be found who saw either of them. The murderer would seem to have been only a few minutes in the City, having just come from Berners Street & returned at once to Whitechapel via Goulston Street where the apron was found.

On the 16th Inst, Mr. Lusk, No. 1 Alderney Road, Mile End, Chairman of the East End Vigilance Committee

(6)

received by post a packet containing
half of a kidney and a letter ^photograph copy
of which I attach hereto. He did not
attach any importance to it at the
time, but on mentioning the matter
to other members of the Committee
on the 18th Inst, they advised him to
shew the piece of kidney to a
medical man. He accordingly took
it to Dr. Reed, 56 Mile End Road
& subsequently to Dr. Openshaw of
the London Hospital, both of whom
expressed the opinion that it was a
portion of the kidney of a human
being. Dr. Lusk then took the
kidney & letter to Leman Street Station
The kidney was forwarded to this
office & the letter to Scotland Yard
Chief Inspector Swanson having
lent me the letter on the 30th Inst
I had it photographed & returned it
to him on the 31st. The kidney has
been examined by Dr. Gordon-Brown
who is of opinion that it is human
Every effort is being made to trace
the sender, but it is not desirable
that publicity should be given to the
Doctor's opinion, or the steps that

(7)   are

are being taken in consequence.
It might turn out after all, to be the
act of a medical student who would
have no difficulty in obtaining the
organ in question.
    This department is co-operating
with the Metropolitan Police in
the matter, and Chief Inspector
Swanson and I meet daily and
confer on the subject

                    (Sgd) Jas McWilliam
                              Inspector

(8)

THE WRITING ON THE WALL

At around 2.55 a.m., P.C. Alfred Long found the missing portion of Catherine Eddowes's apron in a doorway of Wentworth Model Dwellings on Goulston Street. It was stained with blood and faeces, and the blade of a knife had evidently been wiped on it. Long's first thought was that someone had been attacked and that they could be lying injured or even dead inside the dwellings. So he stood up, intending to search the block and, as he did so, he noticed a scrawled message chalked on to the wall directly above the apron, which read "The Juwes are the men that will not

be blamed for nothing." Moments later, another officer arrived at the scene, and Long asked him to guard the building while he took the portion of apron round to Commercial Street Police Station, where he handed it to an inspector.

Soon, officers of the Metropolitan Police were gathering around the doorway and staring nervously at the graffito. Wentworth Model Dwellings not only stood in a largely Jewish locality, but was also inhabited almost exclusively by Jews. The officers feared that if the message was left, there might be an outbreak of racial unrest in the district. They were therefore anxious to erase the message sooner rather than later.

But detectives from the City Police also began arriving at the scene. They were adamant that the graffito was an important clue in their hunt for the killer of Catherine Eddowes and wanted it photographed. The Metropolitan Police pointed out that this would entail waiting until it was light, by which time Gentile purchasers would be arriving in their thousands to purchase from the Jewish stallholders at the Petticoat Lane and Goulston Street Sunday markets. Since there was no way of keeping it hidden from these crowds, the Metropolitan Police were convinced that the result could be a full-scale anti-Jewish riot. Daniel Halse, of

LEFT Sir Charles Warren inspects the Goulston Street Graffito.

BELOW The City Police were responsible for investigating the murder of Catherine Eddowes.

the City Police, suggested that only the top line, "The Juwes are", should be erased. Superintendent Arnold, of the Metropolitan Police, argued that the context would still remain.

The two forces were still bickering over what should be done when Sir Charles Warren arrived at the scene between 5 and 5.30 a.m. Agreeing with his officers that leaving the graffito would lead to far greater crimes against innocent Jews, he ordered that the message be erased immediately, and before a photograph could be taken. It would prove a highly controversial order, and Major Smith, the acting City Police Commissioner, was barely able to disguise his contempt for Warren's actions in the days and weeks that followed. But Warren was convinced that he had done the right thing and later defended his actions in a report to the Home Office:

"… it was just getting light, the public would be in the streets in a few minutes, in a neighbourhood very much crowded on Sunday mornings by Jewish vendors and Christian Purchasers from all parts of London … The writing was on the jamb of the open archway or doorway visible to anybody in the street and could not be covered up without danger of the covering being torn off at once … after taking into consideration the excited state of the population in London … the strong feeling which had been excited against the Jews, and the fact that in a short time there would be a large concourse of the people in the streets … I considered it desirable to obliterate the writing at once … I do not hesitate myself to say that if the writing had been left there would have been an onslaught upon the Jews, property would have been wrecked, and lives would probably have been lost …"

THE APRON

The journey from Mitre Square to the doorway in Goulston Street, where the portion of apron was discovered, is no great distance and can be walked at a rapid pace in less than 10 minutes. Alfred Long and Detective Constable Daniel Halse had passed the doorway at around 2.20 a.m. and both were adamant that the apron had not been there then. It is possible that they were mistaken and had simply not noticed it. But if they were correct and the apron was not there at that time, then this suggests that the murderer had loitered in the area for anywhere between 35 minutes and an hour, during which time the police were searching for him, and stopping and questioning any man they met.

ABOVE The bloodstained piece of Catherine Eddowes's apron is presented at her inquest.

BELOW The City Police detectives were based in this building in Old Jewry.

93305
28

Confidential

HOME OFFICE
6 NOV 88

4, Whitehall Place.
S.W.

6th November, 1888.

Sir,

In reply to your letter of the 5th instant, I enclose a report of the circumstances of the Mitre Square Murder so far as they have come under the notice of the Metropolitan Police, and I now give an account regarding the erasing the writing on the wall in Goulston Street which I have already partially explained to Mr. Matthews verbally. —

On the 30th September on hearing of the Berners Street Murder

The Under Secretary
of State
to the
Home Office

Murder after visiting Commercial Street Station I arrived at Leman Street Station shortly before 5 am. and ascertained from Superintendent Arnold all that was known there relative to the two murders. —

The most pressing question at that moment was some writing on the wall in Goulston Street evidently written with the intention of inflaming the public mind against the Jews, and which Mr. Arnold with a view to prevent serious disorder proposed to obliterate, and had sent down an Inspector with a sponge for that purpose telling him

to

THIS AND FOLLOWING PAGES Warren's defence of his order to erase the Goulston Street graffito before a photograph of it could be taken.

to await his arrival. —

I considered it desirable
that I should decide this
matter myself, as it was
one involving so great
a responsibility whether any
action was taken or not. —
I accordingly went down
to Goulston Street at once
before going to the scene of
the murder: it was just
getting light, the public
would be in the streets
in a few minutes, in a
neighbourhood very much
crowded on Sunday mornings
by Jewish vendors and
Christian purchasers from

all parts of London.

There were several Police
around the spot when I
arrived, both Metropolitan
and City. —

The writing was on the
jamb of the open archway
or doorway visible to any
body in the street and
could not be covered up
without danger of the covering
being torn off at once. —

A discussion took place
whether the writing could
be left covered up or
otherwise or whether any
portion of it could be
left for an hour until
it could be photographed,
but

but after taking into
consideration the excited
state of the population
in London generally at
the time the strong feeling
which had been excited
against the Jews, and
the fact that in a
short time there would
be a large concourse of

the

the people in the streets and having before
me the Report that if it was left there the
house was likely to be wrecked (in which
from my own observation I entirely concurred)
I considered it desirable to obliterate the
writing at once, having taken a copy of
which I enclose a duplicate.

After having been to the scene of
the murder, I went on to the City Police
Office and informed the Chief Superintendent
of the reason why the writing had been
obliterated.

I may mention that so great
was the feeling with regard to the Jews
that on the 13th ulto. the Acting Chief Rabbi
wrote to me on the subject of the Spelling of
the word "Juewes" on account of a
newspaper asserting that this was Jewish

Spelling

spelling in the Yiddish dialect. He added,
"in the present state of excitement it is
"dangerous to the safety of the poor Jews
"in the East. To allow such an assertion
"to remain uncontradicted. My community truly
"appreciates your humane and vigilant action
"during this critical time."

It may be realised therefore if
the safety of the Jews in Whitechapel Could
be considered to be jeopardised 13 days
after the murder by the question of the spelling
of the word Jews, what might have happened
to the Jews in that quarter had that writing
been left intact.

I do not hesitate myself to say
that if that writing had been left there would
have been an onslaught upon the Jews, property
would have been wrecked, and lives would
probably have been lost; and I was much
gratified

gratified with the promptitude with which
Superintendent Arnold was prepared to act
in the matter if I had not been there.

I have no doubt myself whatever
that one of the principal objects of the Reward
offered by Mr. Montagu was to shew to the
world that the Jews were desirous of having
the Hanbury Street murder cleared up, and
thus to divert from them the very strong
feeling which was then growing up.

I am,
Sir,
Your most obedient Servant,
Warren

THE JACK THE RIPPER LETTERS

On 29 September 1888, the Central News Agency forwarded a letter to the Metropolitan Police that they had received on 27 September. It was written in red ink and its tone was boastful and mocking. After taunting that the police "won't fix me just yet," the writer went on to warn that he was "down on whores and I shant quit ripping them till I do get buckled". Having told how he had "saved some of the proper red stuff in a ginger beer bottle to write with over the last job," he complained that it had gone "thick like glue and I cant use it". After threatening that "the next job" he did he would "clip the ladys ears off and send to the police officers", the writer signed off with the chilling soubriquet "Jack the Ripper".

Initially the police dismissed the letter as a hoax. But, within 24 hours of their receiving it, the murders of Elizabeth Stride and Catherine Eddowes occurred. The letter's warning that "you will soon hear of me with my funny little games" began to seem a little too prophetic, while the threat to "clip the ladys ears off" suggested premeditation in the light of the cuts on Catherine Eddowes's earlobes. As it transpired, her killer had not attempted to remove her ears, but had simply nicked the lobes in the frenzied slashing of his attack. But that knowledge would come with hindsight, and when a postcard was received in the early post on Monday 1 October, referring to the previous letter and boasting of a "double event this time", the police were duty bound investigate the correspondence and, if possible, trace the author or authors.

Thus, both the card and the letter were reproduced on posters and displayed outside police stations asking that anyone who recognized the handwriting should contact the police. By 4 October, facsimiles of them were appearing in newspapers all over the world. Making the correspondence public turned out to be a huge mistake. The police had quickly decided that it was probably a journalistic joke and not the work of the killer. They had also underestimated the allure of the widespread publicity to hoaxers, who began bombarding the authorities with so much Jack the Ripper correspondence that the detectives on the case were almost overwhelmed as they struggled to investigate it.

One such letter was received by Mr George Lusk, the Chairman of the Whitechapel Vigilance Committee, in the evening post on 16 October 1888. Addressed "From Hell", the badly written, misspelled missive came with half a kidney, which the writer claimed he had taken "from one women". Lusk dismissed it as a hoax and put the stinking organ into a drawer while he pondered what to do with it. His friends, however, persuaded him to seek a medical opinion and so the kidney was submitted to Dr Openshaw of the London Hospital, who concluded that it was human and had been preserved in spirits of wine.

Some newspapers, however, misquoted Dr Openshaw as having stated that the kidney was "ginny" and that it had been taken from the body of a woman who had died within the previous three weeks. Openshaw was quick to issue a denial of these press embroideries, while Dr Sedgwick Saunders, the City analyst, issued a statement pointing out that identifying the sex of a kidney was impossible and that gin leaves no renal traces. He concurred with the view expressed by the majority of police officers and doctors who examined the organ that it was in all probability a hoax perpetrated by a medical student.

THOMAS J. BULLING

In 1913, retired Detective Chief Inspector John George Littlechild wrote to George Sims that the general consensus among senior police officers at the time of murders was that Thomas J. Bulling (although Littlechild misspelled his name as Bullen), a journalist at the Central News Agency, was the man responsible for the Dear Boss letter, and therefore creating the name Jack the Ripper. Interestingly, Bulling also forwarded a transcript of a third Jack the Ripper letter to the police, which was dated 5 October. Although he enclosed the envelope, he only sent a handwritten transcript of the letter. It is apparent that the police had by this time come to the conclusion that the letters were hindering rather than helping the investigation and this letter was not made public. Perhaps they were growing suspicious of Bulling?

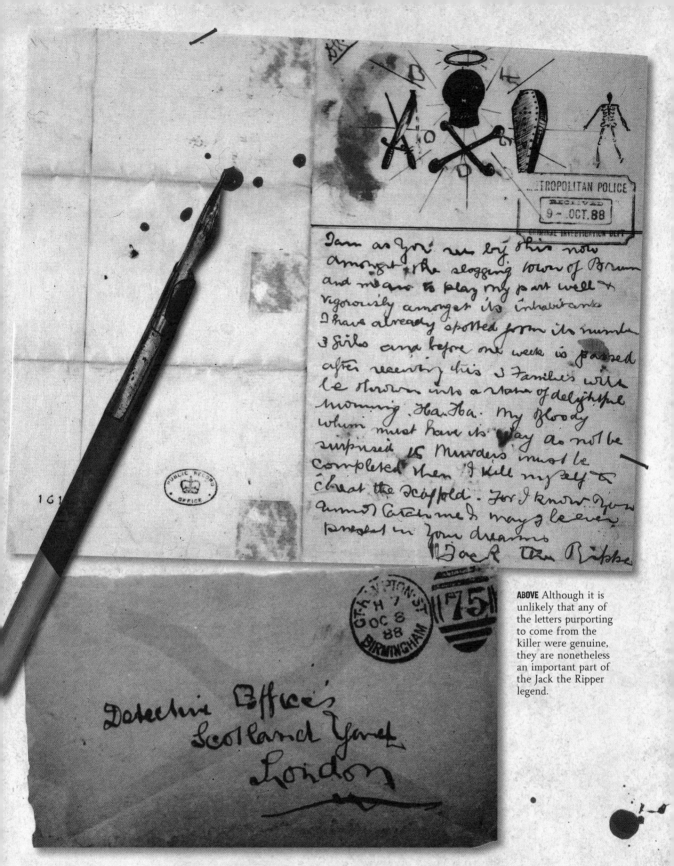

I am as you will by this now amongst the slogging town of Brum and means to play my part well & vigorously amongst its inhabitants I have already spotted from its midst 3 girls and before one week is passed after receiving this 3 families will be thrown into a state of delightful mourning. Ha. Ha. My bloody whim must have its way as not be surprised 15 Murders must be completed then I kill myself to cheat the scaffold. For I know you cannot catch me & may sleep even peaceful in your dreams

Jack the Ripper

ABOVE Although it is unlikely that any of the letters purporting to come from the killer were genuine, they are nonetheless an important part of the Jack the Ripper legend.

Today it is almost universally agreed by historians that neither letter was sent by the person responsible for the murders. But the impact of the "Dear Boss" letter cannot be underestimated, for its arrival in the investigation helped turn a series of sordid East End murders into an international phenomenon, and elevated the unknown miscreant responsible into the realm of enduring legend.

25. Sept: 1888.

Dear Boss.

I keep on hearing the police
have caught me but they wont fix
me just yet. I have laughed when
they look so clever and talk about
being on the right track. That joke
about Leather Apron gave me real
fits. I am down on whores and
I shant quit ripping them till I
do get buckled. Grand work the last
job was. I gave the lady no time to
squeal. How can they catch me
I love my work and want to s
again. You will soon hear of me
with my funny little games. I
saved some of the proper red stuff in
a gingerbeer bottle over the last job
to write with but it went thick
like glue and I cant use it. Red
ink is fit enough I hope ha. ha.
The next job I do I shall clip
the ladys ears off and send to the

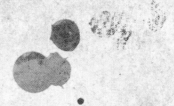

ABOVE AND OPPOSITE The infamous "Dear Boss" letter, received
three days before the double murders of 30 September, marks
the first use of the nom de plume "Jack the Ripper".

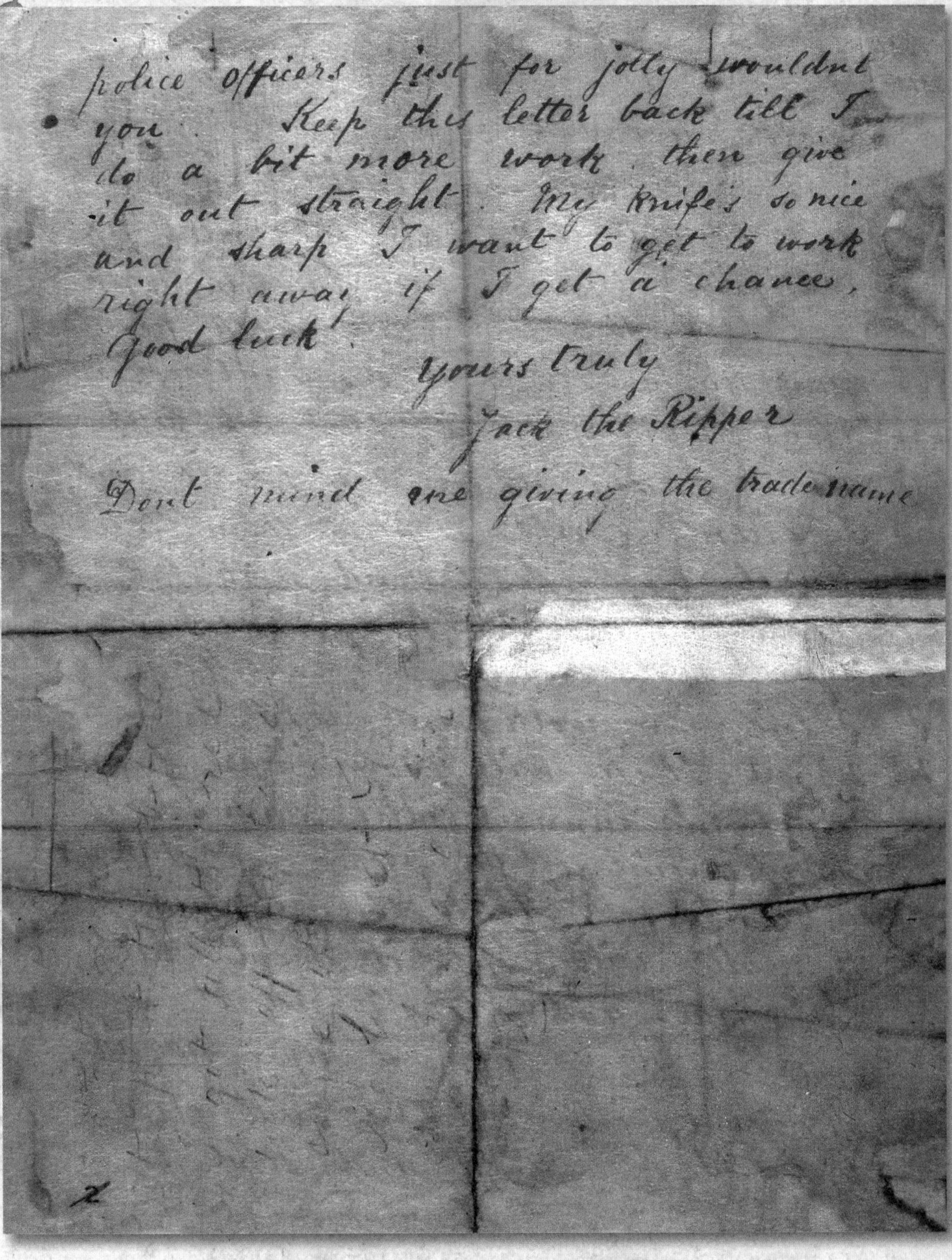

police officers just for jolly wouldnt
you. Keep this letter back till I
do a bit more work, then give
it out straight. My knife's so nice
and sharp I want to get to work
right away if I get a chance,
Good luck

             yours truly

               Jack the Ripper

Dont mind me giving the trade name

2

POST CARD

THE ADDRESS ONLY TO BE WRITTEN ON THIS SIDE

Central News Office
London City

I was not codding
dear old Boss when
I gave you the tip
you'll hear about
saucy Jacky's work
tomorrow double
event this time
number one squealed
a bit couldnt
finish straight
off. had not time
to get ears for
police. thanks for
keeping last letter
back till I got
to work again
Jack the Ripper

ABOVE AND RIGHT The postcard apparently from the same person which speaks of "saucy Jacky's work", a "double event" – the murders of Elizabeth Stride and Catherine Eddowes.

OPPOSITE One of the more illiterate letters, threatening future violence, this one sent directly to pathologist Dr Openshaw.

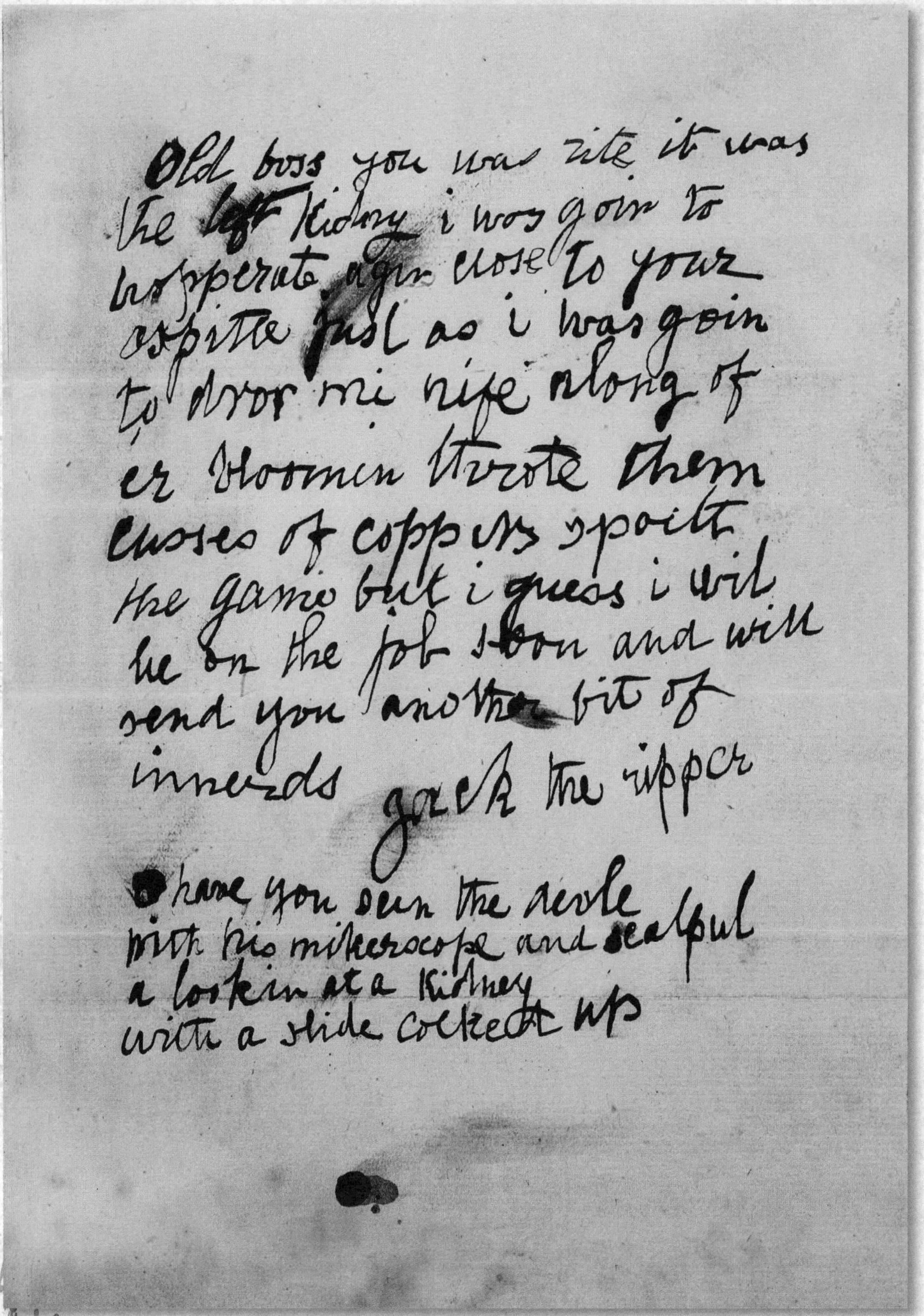

Old boss you was rite it was
the left kidny i was goin to
hoperate agin close to your
ospitle just as i was goin
to dror mi nife along of
er bloomen throte them
cusses of coppers spoilt
the game but i guess i wil
be on the job soon and will
send you another bit of
innerds   jack the ripper

O have you seen the devle
with his mikeroscope and scalpul
a lookin at a kidney
with a slide cocked up

69

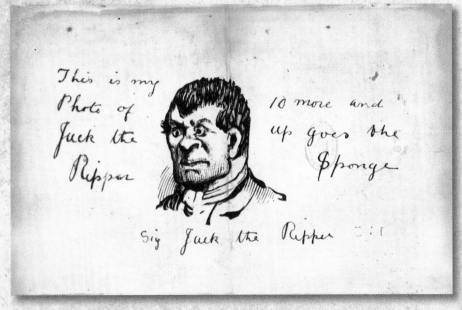

Oct. 10/10

Dear Boss
You will be
Surprised to hear
that you had little
Jacky In your Beb
the other night,
What fun to think
the Police were
Waiting for Me

At the East End
While I was Enjoying
my Little Self good
by You Bet I will
See You beffor Long
I am
your Truly
Jack the
Ripper

This is my
Photo of
Juck the
Ripper

10 more and
up goes the
Sponge

Sig Juck the Ripper

ABOVE A postcard written on 10 October, probably in response to the publicity campaign. This creation features a sketch of the supposed Ripper.

From hell

Mr Lusk
        Sor
I send you half the
Kidne I took from one women
prasarved it for you tother piece
I fried and ate it was very nise. I
may send you the bloody knif that
took it out if you only wate a whil
longer

        Signed   Catch me when
                        you can
                Mishter Lusk —

ABOVE One of the letters sent to Mr
George Lusk addressed "From Hell".

MARY KELLY

For the eight months prior to her death, Mary Kelly had been renting a room at 13 Miller's Court, off Dorset Street in Spitalfields. She shared that room with an unemployed Billingsgate fish porter by the name of Joseph Barnett, but his unemployment had resulted in their falling behind with the rent and Mary had resorted to prostitution. This caused friction between them, and when, in late October 1888, Mary invited a homeless prostitute to stay with them, Barnet moved out, although they remained on friendly terms.

Mary Kelly spent most of her last night imbibing. Her upstairs neighbour, Mrs Anne Cox, saw her around midnight going into her room with a man. She bade her "goodnight", but Mary was drunk and could barely manage a mumbled response.

About 2 a.m. on 9 November, George Hutchinson met Mary on Commercial Street. She asked him for sixpence but he told her he had nothing. Saying that she must find some money, Mary walked on, whereupon a man coming from the opposite direction tapped her on the shoulder and said something to her. They started laughing and the man put his arm around Mary's shoulder, who then led him past Hutchinson and over to Dorset Street. Hutchinson followed and watched as they disappeared into Miller's Court. He waited for about three-quarters of an hour them to re-emerge, and when they did not, he went away.

A little before 4 a.m., several neighbours heard a cry of "Oh Murder!" But, presuming it to be either domestic violence or a drunken brawl, they ignored it.

At 10.45 a.m., Mary Kelly's landlord, John McCarthy, sent his assistant Thomas Bowyer to collect her overdue rent. Getting no reply when he knocked on her door, Bowyer looked through the window and beheld a horrendous sight. Two lumps of flesh lay on the bedside table, while on the bed itself, butchered beyond recognition, he saw the mutilated body of Mary Kelly. Bowyer went to fetch John McCarthy who, having looked into the gloomy

room, pulled back in horror. "The sight we saw I cannot drive away from my mind," he later recalled. "It looked more like the work of a devil than of a man …. I declare to God I had never expected to see such a sight as this … I hope I may never see such a sight again."

Police were soon converging on Miller's Court, and the Divisional Police Surgeon, Dr George Bagster Phillips, arrived at 11.15 a.m. A quick glance through the window was sufficient to satisfy him that the victim was beyond medical help. Inspector Abberline was at the scene by 11.30 a.m., but it would be another two hours before officers entered the tiny room. The delay was caused by a mistaken belief that bloodhounds were to be brought and put on the scent of the killer. However, at 1.30 p.m. Superintendent

Arnold brought news that the bloodhounds were not coming, and he ordered that the door be forced open.

Few officers who saw the awful glut in Miller's Court would ever forget the experience. All the skin had been carved from Mary Kelly's thighs and abdomen. Her abdominal cavity had been emptied of its viscera. The breasts had been cut off, arms mutilated and face hacked beyond recognition. Her neck had been severed down to the bone. The liver lay between her feet; the uterus and kidneys together with one breast were under her head and the other breast was by her right foot; her intestines lay along the right side of her body; and her spleen lay along the left.

Throughout the afternoon, a huge amount of police activity was focused on Miller's Court and the surrounding area. But then, at 4 p.m., a horse and court clattered into Dorset Street and pulled up at the entrance to Miller's Court. Before a crowd of shocked onlookers, a battered coffin was carried out and loaded on to the cart. As men doffed their caps, and women shed silent tears, the body of Mary Kelly was removed to Shoreditch mortuary, and, as darkness descended, wooden boards were nailed across the doors and windows of her room.

RIPPER DESCRIPTION

There is a great deal of debate over George Hutchinson's description of the man with whom he saw Mary Kelly enter Miller's Court. It has been argued that it is far too detailed for a sighting that took place in the darkness of the early hours. So if Hutchinson was lying or exaggerating about what he saw, what was his motivation? One possibility is that he had followed the couple and had, as he said, kept a watch on Miller's Court. When he heard of the murder, he may have panicked that witnesses could have seen him standing there, and to deflect suspicion away from himself, he either invented the man or over-embellished what he had seen. The problem with dismissing Hutchinson's statement outright is that Inspector Abberline, who interviewed him, took it very seriously.

OPPOSITE The Jack the Ripper Murders centred on the area around Commercial Street.

RIGHT Mary Kelly rented a room here in Miller's Court.

BELOW This photograph taken in her room shows the full horror of the injuries inflicted on Mary Kelly.

MORE MURDERS

In the early hours of 20 December 1888, the body of Rose Mylett was found in Clarke's Yard, Poplar. Although her injuries were not suggestive of Jack the Ripper, and she is not generally held to have been one of his victims, her name was included on the list of Whitechapel Murders. However, it would be another seven months before the possibility of the Ripper's return would be raised.

RIGHT Alice McKenzie shown smoking the pipe that gave her the nickname "Claypipe Alice".

BELOW The Princess Alice, one of the pubs that Frances Coles visited with James Thomas Sadler.

At 12.50 a.m. on 17 July 1889, P.C. Walter Andrews was walking his beat along Castle Alley, when he found the still-warm body of prostitute Alice McKenzie lying on the pavement with her throat cut. Her skirts had been raised, exposing her abdomen, along which ran a zig-zag, albeit superficial, wound. The Divisional Police Surgeon, Dr George Bagster Phillips, was summoned and having examined the body, he pronounced life extinct. He later reported that the injuries did not suggest to him that this was the work of Jack the Ripper.

There was, however, disagreement as to whether McKenzie's murder marked the Ripper's return. James Monro, who had taken over as Police Commissioner, was at the scene a little after 3 a.m.. Later that day he informed the Home Office that "every effort will be made … to discover the murderer, who, I am inclined to believe is identical with the notorious 'Jack the Ripper' of last year." Dr Thomas Bond, who examined the body at the mortuary, was also of the opinion that the injuries suggested that this was another Ripper killing. Dr Phillips, however, insisted that the wounds were not severe enough to suggest a Jack the Ripper-style killing.

Dr Robert Anderson, who was away on holiday at the time, later stated that "the murder of Alice McKenzie was by another hand". He even suggested that Monro had later on changed his opinion and come to believe that her murder was "an ordinary murder, and not the work of a sexual maniac".

Two months later, on 10 September 1889, the legless torso of a woman was found beneath a railway arch in Pinchin Street. Although there was a gash across the abdomen, it was soon apparent that this had been inflicted in the course of dismemberment, as opposed to being a deliberate mutilation, and so it was concluded that this was not a Ripper killing.

The final Whitechapel Murders victim was Frances Coles, whose body was found at 12.15 a.m. on 13 February 1891 in Swallow Gardens, a dark passage that ran under a set of railway arches. When Police Constable Thompson found her, blood was still pouring from a savage cut to her throat, and there were signs that she was still alive, although she died soon afterwards.

Police enquiries uncovered the fact that Coles had spent the previous two days in the company of James Thomas Sadler, a somewhat volatile ship's fireman from

ABOVE The mortuary photograph of Frances Coles.

the SS *Fez*. The two had drunk heavily and had argued. When it transpired that, less than an hour after the discovery of Frances Coles's body, Sadler had turned up bloodstained at a lodging house; and that at 10.15 a.m. that morning he had sold his knife to a sailor named Duncan Campbell, the police arrested him and charged him with the murder. Sadler insisted that the bloodstains were the result of his being mugged, but the police were convinced they had their man, and also began looking at the possibility that he could be Jack the Ripper.

But Sadler was able to prove that he had, indeed, been mugged, and that he had not actually been with Frances Coles in the hours before she was murdered. When it was also revealed that his knife was probably too blunt to have inflicted the wound on Coles's throat, the case against him collapsed. He was also able to prove that he had been at sea when some of the other murders had occurred. On 27 February 1891, the jury at the inquest into the death of Frances Coles returned a verdict of murder against some person or persons unknown, and four days later proceedings against Sadler were dropped.

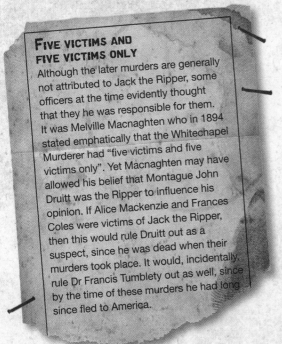

FIVE VICTIMS AND FIVE VICTIMS ONLY

Although the later murders are generally not attributed to Jack the Ripper, some officers at the time evidently thought that they he was responsible for them. It was Melville Macnaghten who in 1894 stated emphatically that the Whitechapel Murderer had "five victims and five victims only". Yet Macnaghten may have allowed his belief that Montague John Druitt was the Ripper to influence his opinion. If Alice Mackenzie and Frances Coles were victims of Jack the Ripper, then this would rule Druitt out as a suspect, since he was dead when their murders took place. It would, incidentally, rule Dr Francis Tumblety out as well, since by the time of these murders he had long since fled to America.

DID JACK THE RIPPER SHOW MEDICAL KNOWLEDGE?

There is considerable debate over whether or not Jack the Ripper demonstrated any medical knowledge in the course of his killings. It was certainly a question that was raised at the inquests into the deaths of the victims, and the majority of the doctors who gave evidence, while generally agreeing that he showed some anatomical knowledge, differed widely as to the degree demonstrated.

Dr Llewellyn, the medic who initially examined Mary Nichols's body, was of the opinion that her killer possessed "some rough anatomical knowledge, for he seemed to have attacked all the vital parts". Wynne Baxter, the Coroner at that inquest, stated in his summing up that the injuries inflicted on both Mary Nichols and Annie Chapman had "in each case been performed with anatomical knowledge".

At Annie Chapman's inquest, Dr George Bagster Phillips, the Divisional Police Surgeon who had examined Annie's body as it lay in the backyard of 29 Hanbury Street, suggested that the mutilations could have been done by "such an instrument as a medical man used for post-mortem purposes ..." However, he also opined that "those used by slaughter-men, well ground down" might just as easily have been used. With regard to the missing womb and other portions of her abdomen, Phillips suggested that the mode in

WOMBS FOR SALE

During his summing-up at Annie Chapman's inquest, Coroner Wynne Baxter caused a sensation by revealing that the sub-curator of a Pathological Museum had informed him of an American doctor who, some months previously, had asked him to procure a number of wombs, for which he was willing to pay £20 each. Apparently, he wished to give them away with copies of a publication that he was working on. The fact that Annie Chapman's womb had been removed raised the possibility, Baxter suggested, that someone might have been influenced to commit the murder in order to acquire the organ for financial gain. His claims were quickly refuted by the medical community, and he seems to have changed his mind, as he did not bring the subject up again.

LEFT Crowds often gathered in the streets to discuss the horror of the Jack the Ripper killings.

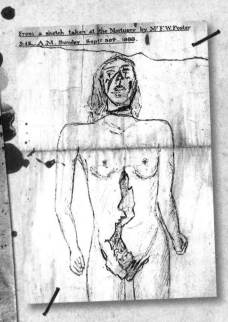

From a sketch taken at the Mortuary by M* F.W. Foster 3.15 A.M. Sunday Sept* 30* 1888.

LEFT This contemporary sketch shows the full extent of Catherine Eddowes's abdominal injuries.

DR PHILLIPS.

RIGHT Dr George Bagster Phillips, the Divisional Police Surgeon.

BELOW A police ambulance of the type used to transport the victims' bodies from the crime scene.

which these had been extracted showed some anatomical knowledge. When recalled to give further medical and surgical evidence by the coroner, Phillips expanded on his earlier testimony and declared that that "the mode in which the knife had been used seemed to indicate great anatomical knowledge."

Summing up at Annie's inquest, Coroner Baxter was adamant that her injuries had been made by someone who "had considerable anatomical skill and knowledge". He went on to say that her womb had been taken by "one who knew where to find it, what difficulties he would have to contend against, and how he should use his knife, so as to abstract the organ without injury to it. No unskilled person could have known where to find it, or have recognized it when it was found …"

At the inquest into the death of Catherine Eddowes, Dr Sequira, the first medical man to examine her body in Mitre Square, expressed the opinion that the murderer possessed no great anatomical skill. In contrast, Dr Frederick Gordon Brown, the City of London Police Surgeon, stated that the person who inflicted the wounds on Catherine Eddowes would have required a good deal of knowledge as to the position of the organs in the abdominal cavity and the way of removing them. He also believed that her murderer would have required a "great deal of knowledge" as to the position of her left kidney in order to have removed it. But such knowledge, he stated, could have been possessed by someone accustomed to cutting up animals.

The final medical man to express an opinion on the question of anatomical knowledge at Catherine Eddowes's inquest was Dr William Sedgwick Saunders, who had assisted at her post-mortem. He was adamant that the wounds showed no sign of having been inflicted by a person with great anatomical skill.

The main dissenting voice on the issue of the murderer possessing any anatomical or surgical knowledge was that of Dr Thomas Bond, the Police Surgeon for the Metropolitan Police's A Division, who, in the aftermath of Mary Kelly's death, prepared a report on all the murders. According to Bond, the mutilations were inflicted "… by a person who had no scientific nor anatomical knowledge … [not even] the technical knowledge of a butcher or horse slaughterer or any person accustomed to cut up dead animals."

So, with the exception of Dr Thomas Bond, all the doctors who had examined the victims' bodies were of the opinion that a basic grasp of anatomy was demonstrated by the killer, although their opinions differed as to the depth of his anatomical knowledge.

the the inc

THOMAS CUTBUSH AND THE MACNAGHTEN MEMORANDUM

Thomas Cutbush was a violent lunatic who was almost certainly not Jack the Ripper. Yet his name is important because, without him, there is a good chance that a document which has formed the bedrock of modern Ripper studies, setting the canonical number of his victims at five and naming three major suspects, would never have been written.

On 13 February 1894, the *Sun* newspaper began a series of articles in which it claimed to know the identity of Jack the Ripper. Although the *Sun* never actually named its suspect, it was apparent that the articles were referring to Thomas Hayne Cutbush, who had been detained as a wandering lunatic at Lambeth Infirmary on 5 March 1891.

Within hours of being admitted, he escaped and, while at large, stabbed Florence Grace Johnson and attempted to stab another woman, Isabelle Frazer Anderson. He was arrested on 9 March 1891 and the following month he was declared insane and sent to Broadmoor Criminal Lunatic Asylum.

There he would have doubtless been forgotten, had the *Sun* not begun its series of sensational articles that apparently ruffled more than a few official feathers. Thomas Cutbush was the nephew of a senior Metropolitan Police Officer, Executive Superintendent Charles Cutbush, and it seems that the authorities became concerned that the fact he was related to a senior

BELOW Thomas Cutbush was sent to Broadmoor Criminal Lunatic Asylum.

he was not Jack the Ripper. Having done so, he went on to state emphatically that "the Whitechapel Murderer had five victims and five victims only", thus establishing the so-called "canonical" five victims. Macnaghten also expressed his certainty about what became of the murderer:

"It will be noted that the fury of the mutilations increased in each case, and, seemingly, the appetite only became sharpened by indulgence. It seems, then, highly improbable that the murderer would have suddenly stopped in November '88 … A much more rational theory is that the murderer's brain gave way altogether after his awful glut in Miller's Court, and that he immediately committed suicide, or, as a possible alternative, was found to be so hopelessly mad by his relations, that he was by them confined in some asylum."

ABOVE Melville Macnaghten, the man who named three major suspects in his memorandum written in 1894.

police officer might lead to accusations of an official cover-up. Questions may have been asked in Parliament and, for that reason, the Chief Constable of Scotland Yard, Sir Melville Leslie Macnaghten, was either asked by his superiors or else undertook of his own volition to prepare a document in which he refuted the Sun's claims.

That document, now known as the Macnaghten Memorandum, was rediscovered in the late 1950s, and it contains several statements that have since formed a basis for the majority of historical studies and accounts of the Whitechapel Murders.

Although conceding that Cutbush's whereabouts on the nights of the murders were unknown, Macnaghten exposed several glaring errors and inconsistencies in the Sun's allegations, proving beyond reasonable doubt that

Finally, Macnaghten mentioned the names of three suspects "any one of whom would have been more likely than Cutbush" to have been the murderer. This assertion has frequently been misinterpreted as Macnaghten's naming the police's three leading suspects. But this, quite clearly, is not the case. He simply stated that any one of these three men was as likely to have been the murderer as Cutbush. Furthermore, it should be remembered that the memorandum merely contains Macnaghten's own personal opinion as to the fate and identity of the murderer. He had joined the force at a time when the hunt for Jack the Ripper was still active. There can be little doubt that the police at the time were monitoring asylum admissions and suicides for clues to the Ripper's fate and identity. Macnaghten would have been privy to all the information that the police received, so when he sat down to refute the accusations against Cutbush, he may well have used this inside knowledge to identify three suspects who, in his opinion, were more likely to have been Jack the Ripper. Since he was a senior officer, and most certainly knowledgeable about the case, any investigation of potential suspects must begin with the three names contained in his memorandum.

ABOVE New Scotland Yard, the headquarters of the Metropolitan Police when Macnaghten wrote his memorandum.

CHARLES HENRY CUTBUSH (1844-96)

Superintendent Cutbush, the uncle of Thomas Cutbush, was in charge of pay and supplies at Scotland Yard. By the mid 1890s, he was displaying mild paranoid delusions, complaining of headaches (apparently brought on by a head injury as a result of a fall) and suffering with depression as a result of his health problems. In March 1896, while sitting one afternoon with his daughter Ellen in his drawing room, he committed suicide by shooting himself in the head. The jury at his inquest returned a verdict of suicide while temporarily insane.

The case, referred to in the sensational story told in "the Sun" in its issue of 13th inst, & following dates, is that of Thomas Cutbush who was arraigned at the London County Sessions in April 1891, on a charge of maliciously wounding Florence Grace Johnson, & attempting to wound Isabella Fraser Anderson in Kennington. He was found to be insane, and sentenced to be detained during Her Majesty's pleasure.

This Cutbush, who lived with his mother and aunt at 14 Albert St, Kennington, escaped from the Lambeth Infirmary, (after he had been detained there only a few hours, as a lunatic) at noon on 5th March 1891. He was recaptured on 9th idem. A few weeks before this, several cases of stabbing, or "jobbing" girls behind had occurred in the vicinity, and a man named Colicott was arrested, but subsequently discharged owing to faulty identification. The cut in the girls' dresses made by Colicott were quite different to the cut made by Cutbush (when he wounded Miss Johnson) who was no doubt influenced by a wild desire of morbid imitation. Cutbush's antecedents were enquired into by Ch: Inspr. (now Supt) Chisholm, by Inspr. Race, and by P.S. McCarthy C.I.D. (the last named officer had been specially employed in Whitechapel at the time of the murders there,) and it was ascertained that he was born, & had lived, in Kennington all his life. His father died when he was quite young, and he was always a "spoilt" child. He had been employed as a clerk,

and traveller in the Tea trade at the Minories, & subsequently canvassed for a Directory in the East End, during which time he bore a good character. He apparently contracted syphilis about 1888, and, - since that time, - led an idle and useless life. His brain seems to have become affected, and he believed that people were trying to poison him. He wrote to Lord Grimthorpe, and others, - & also to the Treasury, - complaining of Dr. Brooks, of Westminster Bridge Rd, whom he threatened to shoot for having supplied him with bad medicines. He is said to have studied medical books by day, & to have rambled about at night, returning frequently into his clothes covered with mud; but little reliance could be placed on the statements made by his mother or his aunt. The latter appears to have been of a very excitable disposition. It was found impossible to ascertain his movements on the nights of the Whitechapel murders. The knife found on him was bought & Houndsditch about a week before he was arrested in the Infirmary. Cutbush was a nephew of the late Supt Executive.

Now the Whitechapel murderer had 5 victims - & 5 victims only, - his murders were

(i) 31st Aug '88. Mary Ann Nichols - at Bucks Row, who was found with her throat cut - & with (slight) stomach mutilation.

(ii) 8th Sept '88. Annie Chapman - Hanbury St: throat cut - stomach & private parts badly mutilated & some of the entrails placed round the neck.

(iii) 30th Sept '88. Elizabeth Stride - Berner's Street

throat cut, but nothing in 'shape of mutilation
attempted. + on same date

Catherine Eddowes. Mitre Square. throat cut.
injury had mutilation, both of face estranced.
(&)
9th November. Mary Jane Kelly. Miller's Court
throat cut, and the whole of the body mutilated
in the most ghastly manner.

The last murder is the only one that took
place in a room, and the murderer must
have been at least 2 hours engaged. A photo
was taken of the woman, as she was found
lying on the bed, without seeing which it
is impossible to imagine the awful mutilation

With regard to the double murder which
took place on 30th Sept., there is no doubt
but that the man was disturbed by some
Jews who drove up to a Club, (close to
which the body of Elizabeth Stride was
found) and that he then, 'mordum satietis',
went in search of a further victim whom
he found at Mitre Square.

It will be noticed that the fury of the
mutilations increased in each case, and,
seemingly, the appetite only became sharpened
by indulgence. It seems, then, highly improbable
that the murderer would have suddenly
stopped in November '88, and been content
to recommence operations by merely prodding
a girl behind some 2 years & 4 months
afterwards. A much more rational
theory is that the murderer's brain gave
way altogether after his awful glut in
Miller's Court, and that he immediately
committed suicide, or, as a possible alternative,
was found to be so hopeless mad by his
relations that he was by them confined in

some asylum.

No one ever saw the Whitechapel murderer;
many homicidal maniacs were suspected, but
no shadow of proof could be thrown on any
one. I may mention the cases of 3 men,
any one of whom would have been more
likely than Cutbush to have committed this
series of murders:—

(1) A Mr M. J. Druitt, said to be a doctor &
of good family, who disappeared at the time
of the Miller's Court murder, whose body
(which was said to have been upwards of
a month in the water) was found in the
Thames on 31st Dec.— or about 7 weeks after
that murder. He was sexually insane and
from private info I have little doubt but
that his own family believed him to have
been the murderer.

(2) Kosminski—a Polish Jew—resident in
Whitechapel. This man became insane owing
to many years indulgence in solitary vices.
He had a great hatred of women, specially of
the prostitute class, and had strong homicidal
tendencies; he was removed to a lunatic asylum
about March 1889. There were many circs
connected with this man which made him
a strong "suspect".

(3) Michael Ostrog, a Russian doctor, and a
convict, who was subsequently detained in a
lunatic asylum as a homicidal maniac.
This man's antecedents were of the worst
possible type, and his whereabouts at the
time of the murders could never be ascertained.

And now with regard to the few of the

inaccuracies and misleading statements made by the "Sun". In its issue of 14th. Feb, it is stated that the writer has in his possession a fac simile of the knife with which the murders were committed. This knife (which for some unexplained reason has, for the last 3 years, been kept by Inspr. Race, instead of being sent to 'Prisoners' Property Store') was traced, & it was found to have been purchased in Houndsditch in Feb. '91, or 2 years & 3 months after the Whitechapel murders ceased!

The statement, too, that Cutbush "spent a portion of the day in making rough drawings of the bodies of women, & of their mutilations" is based solely on the fact that 2 scribble drawings of women in indecent postures were found torn up in Cutbush's room. The head & body of one of these had been cut from some fashion plate, & legs were added to show a woman's naked thighs & pink stockings.

In the issue of 9th. inst it is said that a light overcoat was among the things found in Cutbush's house, and that a man in a light overcoat was seen talking to a woman at Backchurch Lane whose body with arms attached was found in Pinchin St. This is hopelessly incorrect! On 10th. Sept. '89 the nude body, with arms, of a woman was found wrapped in some sacking under a Railway arch in Pinchin St: the head & legs were never found nor was the woman ever identified. She had been killed at least 24 hours before the remains (which had seemingly been brought from a distance)

were discovered. The stomach was split up by a cut, and the head and legs had been severed in a manner identical with that of the women whose remains were discovered in the Thames, in Battersea Park, & on the Chelsea Embankment on 4th June of the same year; and these murders had no connection whatever with the Whitechapel horrors. The Rainham mystery in 1887, & the Whitehall mystery (when portions of a woman's body were found under what is now New Scotland Yard) in 1888 were of a similar type to the Thames & Pinchin St crimes.

It is perfectly untrue to say that Cutbush stabbed 6 girls behind. This is confounding his case with that of Colicott.

The theory that the Whitechapel murderer was left-handed, or, at any rate, "ambi-dexter", had its origin in the remark made by a doctor who examined the corpse of one of the earliest victims; other doctors did not agree with him.

With regard to the 4 additional murders ascribed by the writer in the Sun to the Whitechapel fiend:—

(1) The body of Martha Tabram, a prostitute was found on a common stair case in George Yard buildings on 7th. August 1888; the body had been repeatedly pierced, probably with a bayonet. This woman had, with a fellow prostitute, been in company of 2 soldiers in the early part of the evening: these men were arrested, but the second prostitute failed or refused to identify, and the soldiers were accordingly discharged.

(2) Alice McKenzie was found with her throat cut (or rather _stabbed_) in Castle Alley on 17th July 1889; no evidence was forthcoming, and no arrests were made in connection with this case. The stab in the throat was of the same nature as in the case of the number

(3) Frances Coles, in Swallow Gardens, on 13th February 1891 - for which Thomas Sadler, a fireman, was arrested, &, after several remands, discharged. It was ascertained at the time that Sadler had sailed for the Baltic on 19th July '89, & was in Whitechapel on the nights of 17th idem. He was a man of ungovernable temper & entirely addicted to drink, & the company of the lowest prostitutes.

(4) The case of the unidentified woman whose trunk was found in Pinchin St: on 10th Sepr 1889 - which has already been dealt with.

M L Macnaghten
23rd Feb. 1874

ABOVE AND PREVIOUS PAGES Macnaghten's report on the likelihood of Thomas Cutbush's having been Jack the Ripper.

MONTAGUE JOHN DRUITT

The first name on Macnaghten's list of three suspects is that of M.J. Druitt who, according to Macnaghten, was:

"... said to be a doctor & of good family, who disappeared at the time of the Miller's Court murder, whose body (which was said to have been upwards of a month in the water) was found in the Thames on 31st Dec, or about 7 weeks after that murder. He was sexually insane and from private info I have little doubt but that his own family believed him to have been the murderer."

Montague John Druitt was a barrister who also worked as an assistant schoolmaster at Mr George Valentine's boarding school in Blackheath. At the end of November 1888, he was suddenly dismissed from the school for unspecified "serious trouble". On 31 December, his body was found floating in the Thames at Chiswick. The jury at his inquest returned a verdict of suicide by drowning "whilst of unsound mind".

On the face of it, the case against Druitt is a compelling one. He was, after all, the favoured suspect of Melville Macnaghten. The timing of his suicide would explain the sudden cessation of the crimes, and if Macnaghten is to be believed, his own family even suspected him of being the murderer.

But, on closer inspection, the case against Druitt is a weak one, and Macnaghten is wrong in several of his facts about him. For a start, Druitt was not a doctor, although he did come from a family of doctors. Furthermore, he was 31 at the time of his death, not 41 as Macnaghten stated.

RIGHT Jack the Ripper suspect Montague John Druitt.

ABOVE Montague John Druitt had chambers here on King's Bench Walk in the Inner Temple, London.

Macnaghten was also influenced by his belief that "... the murderer's brain gave way altogether after his awful glut in Miller's Court, and that he immediately committed suicide ..." Druitt's mind most certainly did not give way after the murder of Mary Kelly and he did not immediately commit suicide. Indeed, he was pursuing his duties as a barrister in the week after Mary Kelly's death, and he continued working at Valentine's School until his dismissal on 30 November. Since he probably committed suicide around that time, it would seem likely that he killed himself in reaction to his dismissal.

The most compelling evidence for Druitt's guilt is the fact that his own family apparently believed him to have been the murderer. But Macnaghten does not say that they had any proof that he was, merely that they harboured suspicions about him. It does not

necessarily follow that those suspicions were correct. Furthermore, Macnaghten does not state that it was Druitt's family that told him of these suspicions, but rather that "from private information I have little doubt that his family believed him to be the murderer ..." This private information may, therefore, have been little more than third-hand hearsay.

The biggest objection to Druitt as a viable suspect is that Inspector Abberline most certainly did not think he was the Ripper. In an interview with the *Pall Mall Gazette* in 1903, Abberline is quoted as saying: "I know all about that story. But what does it amount to? Simply this. Soon after the last murder in Whitechapel, the body of a young doctor was found in the Thames, but there is absolutely nothing beyond the fact that he was found at that time to incriminate him."

Finally, nothing that is known about Druitt suggests that he ever visited Whitechapel, nor that he had any knowledge of the area.

As a result of Macnaghten's suspicions, Druitt is commonly placed high up on the list of Ripper suspects. Yet the case against him is dependent on Macnaghten's possessing more information than he wished to reveal – information that he claimed he had destroyed so as not to cause uproar.

Montague John Druitt may have been Jack the Ripper. But equally, he may have simply been a tragic figure who, in taking his own life at around the time that the murders ended, ensured that his name came to the attention of the police as they desperately sought an explanation of the fate of the Whitechapel Murderer.

SUICIDE NOTE

Druitt's body was fished out of the River Thames at Chiswick on 31 December 1888. At the inquest, his brother William, a Bournemouth solicitor, said that he had been told by a friend on 11 December that Montague had not been heard of at his chambers for more than a week. William therefore went to London to make inquiries and discovered that his brother had got into serious trouble at the school and had been dismissed on 30 December. He therefore had Montague's possessions searched and found a paper addressed to him [William]. The letter was produced at Montague's inquest, and its contents revealed the torment of his final days. It read: "Since Friday I felt I was going to be like mother, and the best thing for me was to die." His mother, the inquest was told, had become insane the previous July.

ABOVE The grave of Montague John Druitt.

OPPOSITE The inquest into Druitt's death was held at the Lamb and Tap pub in Chiswick.

RIGHT Druitt's body was found in this picturesque reach of the River Thames at Chiswick.

AARON KOSMINKSI

The second name to appear on the memorandum is that of Kosminski who, according to Macnaghten, was "... a Polish Jew, & resident in Whitechapel. This man became insane owing to many years indulgence in solitary vices. He had a great hatred of women, specially of the prostitute class, & had strong homicidal tendencies; he was removed to a lunatic asylum about March 1889 ..."

Kosminski is of particular interest because, in addition to Melville Macnaghten, the two highest-ranking police officers with direct responsibility for the Jack the Ripper investigation also considered him the murderer.

In 1910, Sir Robert Anderson, Assistant Commissioner throughout the murders, wrote in his memoirs that "... 'undiscovered murders' are rare in London, and the 'Jack-the-Ripper' crimes are not in that category ... I will merely add that the only person who had ever had a good view of the murderer unhesitatingly identified the suspect the instant he was confronted with him; but he refused to give evidence against him ... In saying that he was a Polish Jew I am merely stating a definitely ascertained fact ..."

Although Anderson didn't name this suspect, it is apparent that he was referring to Macnaghten's Kosminski, a fact confirmed in 1987 when Chief Inspector Donald Swanson's copy of Anderson's memoir was made public.

ABOVE Colney Hatch Asylum, to which suspect Aaron Kosminski was sent in 1891.

REGISTRY OF ADMISSIONS—

REGISTER OF PATIENTS.

Swanson was the officer tasked with assessing all the information on the Jack the Ripper case, and few people possessed anything like his comprehensive knowledge of the murders. He and Anderson became firm friends and when *The Lighter Side of My Official Life* was published, Swanson received his own personally inscribed copy.

Swanson made pencilled annotations to Anderson's narrative, and in so doing provided a little more information. Where Anderson talks of a witness "unhesitatingly identifying the suspect but refusing to give evidence against him", Swanson explains that this was "… Because the suspect was also a Jew … and witness would be the means of murderer being hanged which he did not wish to be left on his mind …"

He goes on to say that, following this identification, the suspect was returned to his brother's house in Whitechapel where the City Police kept him under constant surveillance. A short time later this suspect was taken to Stepney Workhouse and from there was sent to Colney Hatch lunatic asylum where, according to Swanson, he died shortly afterwards. Swanson ends with the emphatic statement that "Kosminski was the suspect."

It is now known that the suspect in question was a man named Aaron Kosminski, a feeble-minded imbecile, who was admitted to Colney Hatch Asylum in February 1891, but who had begun displaying signs of insanity at some stage in the late 1880s. He believed that a higher power spoke to him and controlled his actions, and claimed to know the movements of all mankind. He refused to wash and would not accept food from others, preferring instead to eat from the gutter.

Schizophrenic, delusional, paranoid and incoherent are all characteristics of Aaron Kosminski. But there are numerous arguments against his having been Jack the Ripper. Swanson, apparently, knew little about his fate, as Kosminski did not, as Swanson claimed, die shortly after being admitted to Colney Hatch asylum. In fact, he lived for many years, transferring to Leavesden Asylum in 1894, where he died in 1919. Throughout the entire period of his confinement, Aaron Kosminski was never classed as homicidal, and it is specifically stated in his records that he was not a danger to others. Some of his notes state that he was excitable, but the only mention of his being violent was that he once grabbed a chair and made as if to strike an attendant with it.

Anderson and Swanson were the two highest-ranking officers with direct responsibility for the Ripper investigation, and they were both in a position to know the evidence against all the suspects. Yet, unless they are referring to a different Kosminski, or there is more information about him that has yet to come to light, there is little evidence to link Aaron Kosminski to the Jack the Ripper murders.

MONSTER SEEN BY TWO MEN.

ABOVE Kosminski may have been seen with the victims by several witnesses.

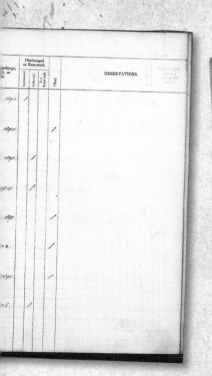

THE MYSTERY WITNESS

There is a great deal of speculation over the identity of the witness who identified Anderson's suspect. However, two possibilities stand out. Anderson wrote that the witness was the only person "who had ever had a good view of the murderer", whilst Swanson added that the witness was Jewish. That would suggest that the witness was either Joseph Lawende, who saw Catherine Eddowes with the man outside Mitre Square, or Israel Schwartz, who witnessed the attack on Elizabeth Stride in Berner Street. Lawende's assertion that he would be unable to recognize the man again would seem to rule him out as the witness. So there is a reasonable chance that the mystery witness was Israel Schwartz.

LEFT The Registry of Admissions to Colney Hatch, showing the name of Aaron Kosminski.

MICHAEL OSTROG

The third and final name on Macnaghten's list of suspects was Michael Ostrog. According to the memorandum, Ostrog was "… a Russian doctor, and a convict who was subsequently detained in a lunatic asylum as a homicidal maniac. This man's antecedents were of the worst possible type, and his whereabouts at the time of the murders could never be ascertained."

Again, Ostrog seems a likely contender but, once more, Macnaghten appears to have known surprisingly little about yet another of his suspects. Ostrog was a petty thief and con artist whose adult years consisted of several long periods of incarceration. His only recorded act of violence in a long criminal career, however, was when he was arrested in 1873 by Police Superintendent Thomas Oswald, on whom he pulled a revolver at the police station.

One newspaper described Ostrog as having "a clever head, a good education and polished manners" and observed that he "would be certain to succeed in almost any honest life to which he might devote himself, but who, nevertheless, is an inveterate criminal …"

BELOW One of the petty thefts carried out by Ostrog was from Eton College.

RIGHT Eton High Street as in the 1880s.

Following a particularly harsh prison sentence of almost ten years for pilfering a few books and a silver cup, the total worth of which was no more than £5, Ostrog was released on 28 August 1883. But by 1887 he was up to his old tricks and he stole a metal tankard from the Royal Military Academy at Woolwich. Apprehended after a chase, he was arrested and committed for trial at the Central Criminal Court, or Old Bailey. During his trial he began to show signs of insanity and, despite the belief of several police officers and doctors that he was "shamming it", he was certified insane and transferred to the Surrey Pauper Lunatic Asylum in Tooting, where his occupation was registered as a Jewish surgeon. He was discharged on 10 March 1888, and as far as the police – to whom he was required to report regularly as a condition of his release – were concerned, he disappeared without a trace.

RIGHT Jack the Ripper suspect Michael Ostrog.

Later that year, at the height of the Ripper scare, when the consensus among the police detectives was that they were looking for a lunatic with medical knowledge, they began looking into all asylum releases that might coincide with the start of the murders. It may have been this search that brought Ostrog's name into the investigation and which later encouraged Macnaghten to include him on his list of three suspects. Certainly, Ostrog's failure to report to the police led to his name and description being published in the *Police Gazette* on 26 October 1888. The description concluded with the warning that "Special attention is called to this dangerous man."

Following another appeal in the *Police Gazette*, Ostrog was apprehended on 17 April 1891. Certified insane, he was sent to Banstead lunatic asylum where it was reported that he was suicidal but not dangerous to others. Significantly, Melville Macnaghten asked the medical officer at Banstead to inform the police if Ostrog was discharged. This happened in 1893, and he promptly returned to a life of thievery, resulting in several more prison terms. He is last heard of being released from prison under licence on 17 September 1904, after which he disappears from the records.

There is nothing in Ostrog's long criminal career to suggest that he was homicidal, and there are no records of his ever attacking women. Furthermore, it seems highly probable that his failure to report to the police following his release from the asylum in March 1888 was because he decided to try his luck in France, where he was arrested under one of his many aliases and held in custody from 26 July 1888 to 18 November 1888, on which date he was brought to trial. Given a two-year prison sentence, he was held in the lunatic wing of a French prison until his release in November 1890. Since this is the crucial period over which the Ripper murders occurred, this would tend to rule him out as a suspect.

BELOW Another of Ostrog's thefts was to steal a tankard from Woolwich Royal Military Academy.

THE STOLEN TANKARD

There is an element of farce about Ostrog's theft of the metal tankard from the Royal Military, Woolwich. Around four o'clock in the afternoon of 19 July 1887, army cadet George Bigge was resting on his bed at the academy, having sprained his ankle. The door opened and Ostrog crept into the room. Having failed to notice Bigge, he proceeded to steal the tankard from the mantelpiece and left. Bigge limped after him, and managed to knock him down. Ostrog got up, and having abandoned his bag, ran off with a group of cadets in hot pursuit. Caught, he was handed over to a police constable, and, while in police custody, he twice attempted suicide.

GEORGE CHAPMAN

George Chapman, born Severin Klosowski, qualified as a junior surgeon in Poland in 1887. Later that year, or early the next, he came to London and found work as an assistant hairdresser. In October 1889, he married Lucy Baderski and by 1890 was working at a barber's shop in the basement of the White Hart pub in George Yard, off Whitechapel High Street. The couple moved to America in 1891 where he established himself as a barber in Jersey City. Following a violent argument, a now pregnant Lucy returned to England where, on 15 May 1892, she gave birth to a baby girl. A few weeks later, Klosowski also returned to London and the couple were briefly reunited. But in 1893, he found another woman, coincidentally named Annie Chapman, and they lived together until she left him in 1894. Klosowski, however, acquired a lasting keepsake from the relationship, for he adopted her name, and from then on was known as George Chapman.

His next lover was Mary Spink, whom he claimed to have married. However, she died on Christmas Day 1897. His next wife, Bessie Taylor, fared little better and died on 13 February 1901. Unperturbed, Chapman married again, but when this wife, Maud Marsh, also died, on 22 October 1902, her family sought the opinion of their own doctor, who became suspicious. The bodies of two of his previous wives were exhumed and significant traces of poison were found. Chapman was arrested, found guilty of murder and executed on 7 April 1903.

BELOW LEFT The White Hart pub, in the cellar of which George Chapman worked as a barber in 1890.

BELOW George Chapman, Inspector Abberline's favoured suspect for the mantle of Jack the Ripper.

Following his conviction, there were suggestions in the press that he might also have been the Whitechapel Murderer. So a journalist from the *Pall Mall Gazette* sought the opinion of the by-then retired Inspector Frederick George Abberline. Abberline admitted that he had never harboured any suspicions against Chapman in relation to the Jack the Ripper murders until the Attorney General made his opening statement at his trial. Since then, however, he had been "so struck with the remarkable coincidences in the two series of murders" that he had not been able to "think of anything else for several days past …"

The *Gazette* quoted Abberline as observing that "there are a score of things which make one believe that Chapman is the man …" These included his having studied surgery and the Whitechapel Murders having been, according to Abberline, "the work of an expert surgeon". Abberline was also struck by the facts that Klosowski's arrival in England coincided with the beginning of the murders; that on arrival he lodged in George Yard, where the first murder was committed; and that the murders ceased in London when Chapman went to America, "while similar murders began to be perpetrated in America after he landed there".

However, Abberline is wrong in a lot of what he says about Chapman. Although Chapman did have surgical training, there is considerable debate over whether or not the Ripper possessed surgical knowledge, and the murders cannot, by any stretch of the imagination, be described as the work of an "expert surgeon". Although Chapman arrived in London around the time that the murders began, so did thousands of other immigrants. Chapman did not begin working in the White Hart

ABOVE The offices of the *Pall Mall Gazette*. A journalist from the publication wrote of Abberline's suspicions concerning Chapman.

pub in George Yard until 1890, around two years after the first murder. Although the murders did cease once Chapman had left for America, this could easily have been coincidence. Moreover, no similar series of murders coincided with his arrival there.

The major objection against Chapman has to be that a killer who could brutally eviscerate his victims with the frenzied violence shown by Jack the Ripper is highly unlikely to have turned to wife-poisoning as a means of venting his homicidal fury. Even though, as Abberline's pointed out, a "… man who could watch his wives being slowly tortured to death by poison, as he did, was capable of anything …" it seems improbable that Chapman was Jack the Ripper.

CARRIE BROWN

Despite Abberline's contention that "similar murders were perpetrated in America after Klosowski landed there", research has established that there were no Ripper-like murders in or around New York during his time there. The only possible crime that could have fallen into this category was the murder of Carrie Brown, whose body was discovered in a room of the East River Hotel, Manhattan, on the night of 23/24 April 1891. Her body had been mutilated, although details of the injuries were suppressed. However, hers appears to have been a one-off murder. So, regardless of whether or not the Ripper killed her, the slaying was not part of series.

METROPOLITAN POLICE.

CENTRAL OFFICER'S
SPECIAL REPORT.

CRIMINAL INVESTIGATION DEPARTMENT,
SCOTLAND YARD,

13th day of November 1888

SUBJECT Whitechapel
Murders

"

REFERENCE TO PAPERS.
52983

I beg to report
that an inquest was held
this day at the Shoreditch
Town Hall before Dr Macdonald
M.P. Coroner on the body of
Marie Jeneatte Kelly, found
murdered at No 13 Room,
Millers Court, Dorset Street,
Spitalfields. A number of
witnesses were called who
clearly established the
identity of deceased
The Coroner remarked
that in his opinion it was
unnecessary to adjourn the
inquiry, and the jury returned
a Verdict of "Wilful Murder
against Some person or
persons unknown".

An important Statement
has been made by a man
named George Hutchinson
which I forward herewith.
I have interrogated him
this evening and I am
of opinion his Statement

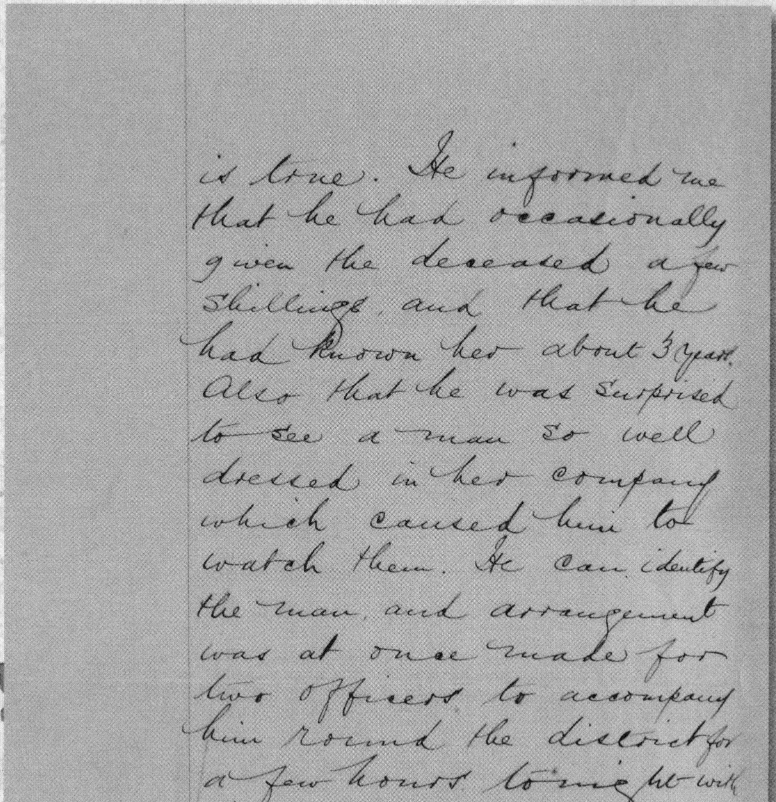

is true. He informed me that he had occasionally given the deceased a few shillings, and that he had known her about 3 years. Also that he was surprised to see a man so well dressed in her company which caused him to watch them. He can identify the man, and arrangement was at once made for two officers to accompany him round the district for a few hours tonight with a view of finding the man if possible.

Hutchinson is at present in no regular employment, and he has promised to go with an officer tomorrow morning at 11.30. am to the Shoreditch Mortuary to identify the deceased.

Several arrests have been made on suspicion of

(2)

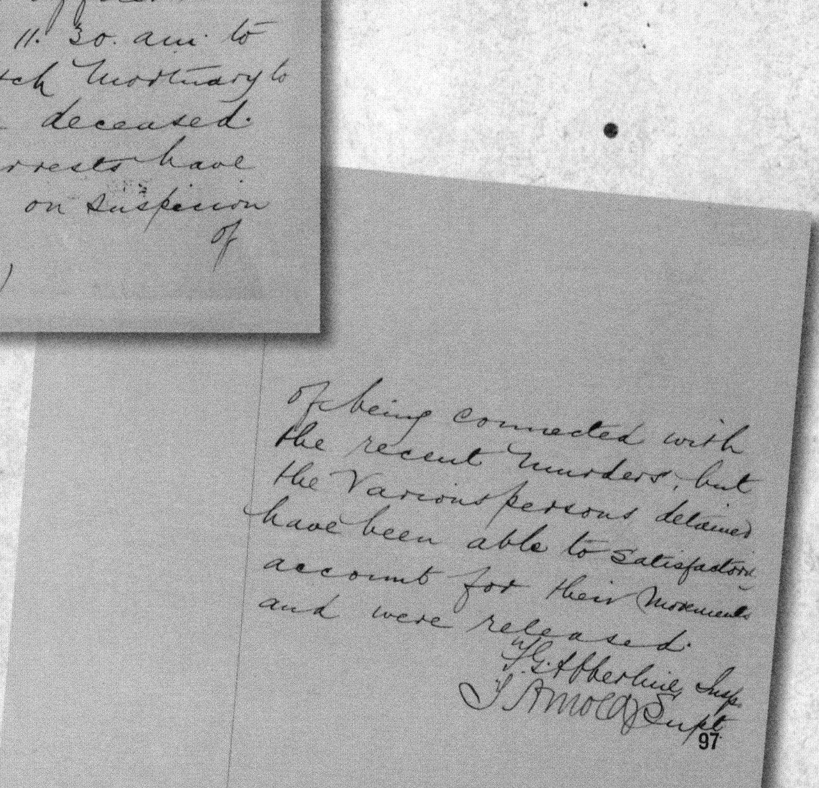

of being connected with the recent murders; but the various persons detained have been able to satisfactorily account for their movements and were released.

F.G. Abberline Insp

T Arnold Supt

THIS PAGE AND OPPOSITE Inspector Abberline's report on the murder of Mary Kelly.

Commercial Street

Metropolitan Police.

No. 6.

Special Report.

H Division.

12 November 1888

Reference to Papers.

Re Murder

At 6 pm 12th George Hutchinson of the Victoria Home Commercial Street came to this Station and made the following statement

About 2 am 9th I was coming by Thrawl Street Commercial Street. and just before I got to Flower and Dean Street. I met the murdered woman Kelly. and she said to me Hutchinson will you lend me sixpence. I said I cant I have spent all my money going down to Romford. she said good morning I must go and find some money. she went away toward Thrawl Street. a man coming in the opposite direction to Kelly tapped her on the shoulder and said something to her they both burst out laughing. I heard her say alright to him. and the man said you will be alright. for what I have told you. he then placed his right hand around her shoulders. He also had a kind of a small parcel in his left hand. with a kind of a strap round it. I stood against the lamp of the Queens Head Public House and watched him. They both then came past me and the man he down his head with his hat over his eyes. I stooped down and looked him in the face. He looked at me

George Hutchinson

C. O. REFERENCE. | DIVISIONAL ...

53,983 | 68

Submitted through

H Division

Subject Re Murder

George Hutchi...

Victoria Home

Commercial...

Description of ...

seen with the m...

woman Marie J...

Kelly at 2 am ...

Metropolitan Police.

No. 6.

Special Report.

H Division.

12th November 1888

Reference to Papers.

Continued

Stern. They both went into Dorset
Street I followed them. they both
stood at the Corner of the Court. for
about 3 minutes. He said something
to her. she said alright my dear
come along you will be Comfortable
He then placed his Arm on her shoulder
and gave her a kiss. She said she had
lost her handkerchief. he then pulled
his handkerchief a red one out and
gave it to her. they both then went up
the Court together. I then went to the
court to see if I could see them but
could not I stood there for about
three quarters of an hour. to see if they
came out they did not so I went away

Circulated
to A.S.

Description age about 34 or 35. high 5.6
Complexion pale. dark eyes and eye lashes
dark slight moustache. curled up each
end. and hair dark. very surley looking
dress long dark. coat collar and cuffs
trimmed astracan. and a dark jacket
under. light waistcoat. dark trousers
dark felt hat turned down in the middle.
button boots. and gaiters. with white
buttons wore a very thick gold chain.
white linen collar. black tie with horse
shoe pin. respectable appearance

Geo Hutchinson

Metropolitan Police.

Special Report.

H Division.

14th November 188

Reference to Papers.

Reumar

walked very sharp. Jewish appearance
Can be identified

George Hutchinson
E Badham Sergt
G Ellisdon Insp
T Arnold Supt

Submitted FG Abberline Insp

FRANCIS TUMBLETY

In 1993, crime historian Stewart P. Evans purchased a batch of correspondence that had belonged to the journalist George Sims. Among the papers was a letter written in 1913 by Chief Inspector John Littlechild, who at the time of the Jack the Ripper crimes had been head of the Metropolitan Police's Secret Department. Littlechild was responding to an enquiry from Sims asking if he had heard of a "Dr D" (evidently a reference to M.J. Druitt) in connection with the Whitechapel Murders.

Littlechild replied that, although he had never heard of a Dr D, "... amongst the suspects, and to my mind a very likely one, was a Dr T [who] was an American quack named Tumblety." According to Littlechild, Tumblety "was arrested in connection with unnatural offences remanded on bail [he] jumped bail, and got away to Boulogne. He shortly left Boulogne and was never heard of afterwards. It was believed he committed suicide but certain it is that from that time the 'Ripper' murders came to an end."

At first glance, Tumblety is another promising suspect. He was charged with acts of gross indecency with a number of males on 7 November 1888. His arrest and subsequent suicide would explain the sudden cessation of the murders. However, on closer inspection the case against him becomes incredibly flimsy. Contrary

ABOVE It was an enquiry from journalist George Sims that prompted Littlechild to suggest Tumblety as a suspect.

LEFT Detective Littlechild, whose naming of Dr Tumblety introduced historians to a new Ripper suspect.

to Littlechild's assertion that he was "never heard of" after leaving Boulogne, he did, in fact, sail for New York where the American press were soon reporting his possible involvement in the Whitechapel Murders. From the moment he arrived, he was kept under surveillance by Chief Inspector Byrnes of the New York Police. Byrnes is on record as saying that "there is no proof of his [Tumblety's] complicity in the Whitechapel murders, and the crime for which he was under bond in London is not extraditable." Byrnes appears to have doubted Tumblety's guilt and even, according to the *New York Times*, "... laughed at the suggestion that he was the Whitechapel murderer ..."

A claim made by those who favour Tumblety as a suspect is that he collected medical specimens, including uteri. However, there is no proof of this. The allegation that he did was contained in an account given by Colonel C.S. Dunham to the *Williamsport Sunday Grit* in which he told of attending a dinner at which Tumblety had "fiercely denounced all women and especially fallen women". According to Dunham, Tumblety then took his guests to his office where he showed them a dozen or more jars containing the uteri of every class of woman. It should, however, be noted that Dunham's veracity is, to say the least, questionable. He was a known confidence trickster, who only made his claims after press allegations had linked Tumblety to the Whitechapel Murders. There is, therefore, a distinct possibility that he invented the story to cash in on Tumblety's sudden notoriety.

Another oft-quoted piece of evidence against Tumblety is that people who knew him thought he was the killer.

Again, this is mere hearsay. Some of them might have thought so, but others were adamant that he was not. His New York landlady, Mrs McNamara, for example, was quoted in the *New York Herald* as saying that "Dr Tumblety ... is a perfect gentleman. He wouldn't hurt anybody."

The case for Tumblety's having been Jack the Ripper is not a strong one. There is no evidence that he ever visited Whitechapel and he bore no resemblance to witness descriptions of the killer. There is no evidence that he was ever violent and, in this respect, even Littlechild appears to have doubted him as a suspect, since he states in his letter to Sims that Tumblety was "not known as a 'Sadist' (which the murderer unquestionably was)". Furthermore, had the police thought him responsible for the murders it seems highly unlikely that they would have released him on bail. Even if they had, his whereabouts were known to their New York counterparts, who could have arrested and extradited him. The reason this was not done has to have been that he had been ruled out of any involvement in the crimes.

ABOVE Dr Francis Tumblety, another possible contender for the mantle of Jack the Ripper.

SCOTLAND YARD IN NEW YORK

One of the claims made by those who favour Tumbelty as a suspect is that, following his flight from London, Scotland Yard sent a top detective to New York to investigate him. This is not strictly true. What happened was that Inspector Andrews had escorted two criminals to Toronto in early December 1888. By 20 December, he was in Montreal and was questioned by journalists about the Whitechapel Murders. He was emphatic that "the police were without a jot of evidence upon which to arrest anybody". Andrews was then sent to New York, supposedly on Ripper-related business, although what that business was is unknown. It may have been to do with Tumblety, it may not.

RIGHT New York in the 1880s – Tumbelty's place of refuge and the possible scene of a Scotland Yard investigation.

JAMES MAYBRICK

In 1992, Michael Barrett, a former Liverpool scrapmetal merchant, produced a journal which, he claimed, had been given to him by a friend, Tony Devereux, in a pub the previous year. Although the diarist does not actually identify himself by name, from personal references and other information contained in the document it is evident that the reader is intended to deduce that the diary was that of Liverpool cotton merchant James Maybrick, whose wife Florence was accused of poisoning him with arsenic, following his death in May 1889.

In the journal, the author claimed that he witnessed his wife – whom he refers to throughout the diary as "the bitch", or "the whore" – with her unnamed lover in the Whitechapel district of Liverpool. This caused him to vent his pent-up fury by commencing a murder spree which culminated in the killing of five prostitutes in the Whitechapel district of London. The diary gives a rambling account of the murders and ends with the confession, "I give my name that all know of me, so history do tell, what love can do to a gentle man born. Yours truly, Jack the Ripper."

There had never been any suggestion of Maybrick's bein Jack the Ripper until his alleged diary (re-)surfaced in 1992, s the case against him has always depended upon proving that h was indeed the journal's author, a task which has been far fro straightforward.

Initially, several experts who examined the journal agreed tha it was of the right period. However, they stressed that a detaile forensic analysis was necessary to establish exactly when it wa written, and the subsequent scientific evidence has proved, t say the least, contradictory.

The diary's provenance was not helped by the fact tha Michael Barrett later confessed in the *Liverpool Daily Post* tha he had forged it. However, he then retracted his confession, an his estranged wife claimed that her family had possessed it sinc the Second World War.

The diary's provenance and age aside, many of the details tha it contains about the crimes, far from demonstrating first-han knowledge, are evidently gleaned from press reports and late accounts of the murders. As a result, the diary repeats some o the common errors and misconceptions concerning the Jack th Ripper cases and his victims. In Mary Kelly's case, for example the diarist says that he placed parts of her body all over the room

BELOW The court in Liverpool where Florence Maybrick was tried and found guilty of poisoning her husband, James.

and that having cut off her breasts and kissed them for a while, he placed them on the bedside table. The idea of Mary Kelly's body parts being strewn around her room is a common fallacy and is demonstrably untrue. Likewise, her breasts were not placed on the bedside table but were, in fact, found beneath her body. This is just one example of several such fallacies that find their way into the supposed confession, and which cast doubt on the author's viability as a suspect.

There is, however, another intriguing piece of memorabilia that links Maybrick to the Jack the Ripper crimes. In 1993, Albert Johnson purchased an antique gold watch on the inside of which he found scratched the initials of Jack the Ripper's five victims, together with the signature "J. Maybrick" and the words "I am Jack."

As with the diary, the watch has been subjected to scientific analysis and the scratches have been found to be compatible with the period 1888 to 1889, although these findings have been disputed. But the watch's appearance, so soon after the diary was made public, aroused a great deal of suspicion, and, whereas it is possible that they were both created at the same time, their usefulness in proving Maybrick's guilt depends on proving that they are genuine, and this has never been satisfactorily done.

The arguments both for and against the viability of Maybrick as a suspect continue, and the general consensus is that the diary is a forgery – although whether done in the nineteenth or late-twentieth century is still contested. One thing is, however, certain. We have not heard the last of James Maybrick as a Jack the Ripper suspect.

ABOVE James Maybrick, a relatively recent Ripper suspect, who reputedly kept a diary detailing his crimes.

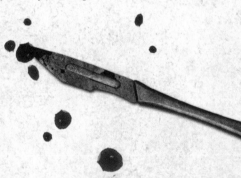

LEFT Florence Maybrick, whose conviction for the murder of her husband, James Maybrick, caused a public outcry.

FLORENCE MAYBRICK
Following James Maybrick's death on 11 May 1889, his American-born wife, Florence, was arrested and charged with his murder. She stood trial at Liverpool Crown Court. Her trial was a travesty. The case against her was extremely weak, and the judge, Mr Justice Stephen, showed considerable animosity toward her, his summing-up including a vitriolic attack on her moral character. She was found guilty and sentenced to death. However, following a huge public outcry on both sides of the Atlantic, her sentence was commuted to one of life imprisonment. She was released in 1904, and lived out the remainder of her years in her native America, where she died in 1941.

THE ROYAL RIPPER AND THE FREEMASONS

Perhaps the most oft-quoted piece of Jack the Ripper misinformation is that he was a member of the royal family, and that the reason he was never caught was because the various British authorities conspired to suppress such an awful and inconvenient truth.

The royal in question was Prince Albert Victor, Duke of Clarence, the grandson of Queen Victoria. According to the theory, Prince Albert had contracted "syphilis of the brain" and the resultant insanity had set him on an East End rampage, murdering and mutilating prostitutes. As a keen deer hunter, so the hypothesis goes, he would have possessed the necessary anatomical knowledge to disembowel his victims, while it has also been noted the Prince bore an uncanny resemblance to another Ripper suspect, Montague John Druitt. This latter point cannot be denied, but a resemblance to another suspect is hardly proof of guilt! That aside, there is no hard historical evidence that in any way links the Prince to the Whitechapel Murders.

On the contrary, his whereabouts at the times of the crimes are well known and they emphatically rule him out as a suspect. On 31 August 1888, the morning that Mary Nichols was murdered, he was staying with Viscount Downe, at Danby Lodge, Grosmont, Yorkshire. On 8 September, the date of Annie Chapman's death, he

BELOW Even Queen Victoria, safely ensconced within Buckingham Palace, was affected by the Ripper crimes.

ABOVE RIGHT Prince Albert Edward Victor, Queen Victoria's grandson and the royal Ripper suspect.

was at the Cavalry Barracks in York. Queen Victoria noted in her journal that she had lunched with him at Abergeldie in Scotland on 30 September, in the early hours of which Elizabeth Stride and Catherine Eddowes had died. Finally, on the day of Mary Kelly's murder, 9 November, he was at Sandringham in Norfolk. So, tempting as it is believe that a syphilitic member of the royal family was Jack the Ripper, there is absolutely nothing that supports such a theory.

Albert Victor's name, however, turns up yet again as part of an even more convoluted, not to say fanciful, theory, which maintains that the killings were nothing less than a Masonic conspiracy to avert a potential royal scandal. The premise behind it is that there had been a secret, and illegal, marriage between Albert Victor and a young Catholic woman named Annie Elizabeth Crook, by whom he had a baby daughter. The fact that an heir to the throne of England had married and sired a child by a Catholic prompted the authorities to act. Annie was incarcerated in a lunatic asylum, where Sir William Gull, Queen Victoria's surgeon, lobotomized her to destroy her memory, thus turning her into a gibbering imbecile who could never be taken seriously in anything she said. But her child's nursemaid, Mary Kelly, fled to the East End, where she fell in with a gaggle of drunken prostitutes, told them what she knew, and together they hatched a plot to blackmail the government.

Robert Cecil, the Prime Minister, a Freemason, enlisted the assistance of fellow Mason Sir William Gull and set him the task of silencing the troublesome crones. Gull inveigled the artist Walter Sickert into the plot, because he knew what Mary Kelly looked like. They were driven round the East End by John Netley, Albert Victor's coachman, and, one by one, the extortionists were hunted down and lured into the royal carriage, where Gull murdered them and mutilated them in accordance with Masonic ritual. Netley then disposed of the bodies at the sites where they were found.

No historical evidence has ever been found that supports the idea of an official conspiracy. It is difficult to believe that, with the number of people involved, some evidence for it would not have surfaced by now. As far as the murders being carried out in a carriage is concerned, the medical evidence disputes this, as it is certain that all of the women died at the spots where their bodies were discovered. Furthermore, the injuries inflicted on the victims were evidently the results of frenzied attacks, not calculated ritual. All in all, the Masonic conspiracy theory is an entertaining hypothesis, but it consists of too much supposition and too many fallacies, not to mention a considerable number of demonstrably disprovable facts that disqualify if from being considered anything like a final solution.

ABOVE Sir William Gull, the royal physician and sometime Ripper suspect.

LEFT Consternation must have run through Freemasons' Hall when the Masons were accused of committing the murders by author Stephen Knight!

JUBELA, JUBELO AND JUBILUM

One aspect of the Masonic conspiracy hypothesis is that the chalked message on the wall in Goulston Street, "The Juwes are the men that will not be blamed for nothing," was a Masonic reference to Jubela, Jubelo and Jubilum, three Masons who murdered their grand master, Hiram Abiff, during the building of Solomon's Temple. Their punishment was to be mutilated in an identical fashion to the injuries suffered by Jack the Ripper's victims. Sir Charles Warren, himself a Freemason, it is alleged, instantly recognized the reference to the Juwes, and so ordered its immediate erasure.

WALTER SICKERT

O ver the years, several authors have linked the artist Walter Sickert to the Whitechapel Murders in a variety of different roles. He has been depicted as an accomplice, an informant and also a theorist. But in 2002, crime novelist Patricia Cornwell, having applied modern forensic techniques to the Jack the Ripper case, caused a worldwide sensation when her book *Portrait of a Killer – Jack the Ripper Case Closed* was published. "I do believe 100 per cent", she told a US chat show, "that Walter Richard Sickert committed those serial crimes …"

The gist of Cornwell's hypothesis is that a series of painful childhood operations for a fistula of the penis had left the adult Sickert impotent, which in turn gave him a pathological hatred of women. The claim has been disputed on the grounds that St Mark's Hospital, at which the operation allegedly took place, specialized in rectal, as opposed to genital, fistulas. Furthermore, it has been pointed out that Sickert's first wife petitioned for divorce on the grounds of his adultery; that he is believed to have had several mistresses; and he was rumoured to have fathered at least one illegitimate son. All of which is hardly suggestive of impotence.

As proof of his pathological hatred of women, Cornwell cites a series of pictures that Sickert painted which were inspired by the murder of Camden Town prostitute Emily Dimmock, in 1907, which she claims bear a striking resemblance to the post-mortem photographs of the Ripper's victims. Sickert was most certainly interested in murder, and in depicting menace, but this hardly makes him guilty of such a crime.

Another major problem with the theory of Sickert's having been Jack the Ripper is that he may not even have been in England when the murders were committed. A number of letters from several family members refer to his holidaying in France during a period that corresponds with most of the Ripper murders. Although it has been suggested that he might have travelled to London in order to commit the murders and then returned to France, no evidence has been produced to suggest that he actually did so.

Cornwell also contends that Sickert was responsible for writing most of the Jack the Ripper correspondence, and frequently uses statements made in those letters to strengthen her case against him. Authorities on the case, as well as the police at the time, nearly all share the opinion that none of the letters – not even the "Dear Boss" missive that gave the Ripper his name – were the work of the killer. In addition, there is the

ABOVE Walter Sickert's name has been put forward as both an accomplice and a leading suspect.

THE RIPPER'S ROOM

Walter Sickert once rented a room that had previously been occupied by Jack the Ripper. At least that is what he alleged his landlady had told him, a few months after he moved in. She went on to reveal that this mysterious lodger was a consumptive veterinary student who used occasionally to stay out all night, and who on returning home around 6 a.m. would burn whatever suit he had been wearing on that particular nocturnal excursion. Eventually, the student's health had given way, and his widowed mother had taken him back to Bournemouth, where he died three months later.

problem that the style of the letters varies so greatly in grammatical structure, spelling and handwriting that it is almost impossible for a single author to have created all of them.

In her quest to prove Sickert's guilt, Cornwell also funded DNA tests on numerous stamps and envelopes which she believed that Sickert had licked, and compared the DNA to that found on the Ripper letters. Interestingly, a possible match was found with the stamp on the Dr Openshaw letter. Critics, however, have pointed out that the DNA comparisons focused on mitochondrial DNA, which could be shared by anything from between one and ten per cent of the population, so it was hardly unique to Sickert.

Another intriguing find was that the Dr Openshaw letter, two other Jack the Ripper letters and eight letters penned by Walter Sickert were all written on paper that bore the watermark of the Aberdeen paper manufacturer Alexander Pirie and Sons. But dissenters argue that the paper was widely available, that the Sickert letters were written between 1885 and 1887, and that he was probably not using that paper in 1888.

Sickert may well have been responsible for writing some of the Jack the Ripper correspondence, but since it is generally agreed that none of it was written by the murderer, it only makes him guilty of having composed hoax letters. The claim that he was also guilty of the Whitechapel Murders is far from proven, and the Jack the Ripper case is anything but closed.

ABOVE Emily Dimmock, whose murder inspired Sickert's paintings, was a well known prostitute in the King's Cross area.

BELOW A favoured haunt of Sickert's was the Rising Sun Pub.

WHY THE RIPPER WAS NEVER CAUGHT

The Victorian police have, over the years, been subjected to a barrage of criticism for their inability to catch Jack the Ripper. Many of the charges levelled against them are largely undeserved, and some of them are downright inaccurate.

For a start, the science of criminal investigation was largely in its infancy at the time. Forensics, offender profiling, DNA profiling, even fingerprinting, were not established methods of crime detection. Furthermore, the murders occurred in one of the most densely populated quarters of London, not to mention a district where a large criminal community had a vested interest in providing as little assistance to the police as possible.

Numerous amateur sleuths were also conducting their own endeavours to bring the killer to justice. But far from helping the police, their activities often had the opposite effect, and came close to overwhelming the investigation with a deluge of bogus information and duff leads. As Inspector Frederick George Abberline later observed, "… we were almost lost in theories; there were so many of them."

The area itself aided the killer's escape from the scenes of his crimes, made up as it was of an intricate warren of alleyways and passages, few of which were lit at night. At the height of the murders, American journalist R. Harding Davis was shown around the area by Inspector Henry Moore. The detective led him through a network of "narrow passageways as dark and loathsome as the great network of sewers that stretches underneath them". Moore told Davis how his men had formed a circle around the spot where one of the murders had taken place "guarding, they thought, every entrance and approach". But within a matter of minutes, they found 50 people inside the circle who had come in through two passageways which, according to Moore "… my men could not find".

The layout of the area might have aided the killer's escapes, but the victims themselves inadvertently provided the perfect locations for his crimes. All but one of those victims conducted their acts of prostitution in the dark courtyards and secluded corners of the neighbourhood. By the very nature of what they did, and the local knowledge required, they knew how to take their murderer to places where there was little danger of interruption. As one police officer put it: "It's not as if he has to wait for his chance, they make that chance for him."

PUNCH, OR THE LONDON CHARIVARI.—September 22, 1888.

BLIND-MAN'S BUFF.

(As played by the Police.)

"TURN ROUND THREE TIMES, AND CATCH WHOM YOU MAY!"

ABOVE This *Punch* cartoon reflects the general consensus that the police were thrashing about in the dark, unable to catch the killer.

It's the Ripper or the Bridge with me

In the wake of each of the Jack the Ripper murders, a wave of panic would grip the neighbourhood and at night people would retreat indoors. The prostitutes would be noticeable by their absence in the immediate aftermath of each murder. But economic necessity would soon force them to venture back out on to the streets and put their lives at risk once more by taking clients into dark corners where the police could not protect them. To cope, they developed a weary acceptance of the danger. In his interview with the American journalist, Inspector Moore told how he would tell the prostitutes to go home. But they would simply reply "… I ain't afraid of him. It's the Ripper or the bridge with me. What's the odds?"

Another major problem faced by the police was that the killer left no clues behind. As Moore confided to Davis: "We have no relics; he never leaves so much as a rag behind him. There is no more of a clue to that chap's identity than there is to the identity of some murderer who will kill someone a hundred years from now."

A frequent bone of contention in the area was that the authorities refused to sanction a reward for information that might lead to the killer's apprehension. The foreman of the jurors at Annie Chapman's inquest even went so far as to express the opinion that the murders of both Nichols and Chapman could have been prevented had a reward been offered in the wake of Martha Tabram's murder. It was, in fact, official government policy not to offer rewards, on the grounds that they simply encouraged people to give false information in the hope of financial gain. It is also worth noting that several private rewards were put up and, following Catherine Eddowes's murder, the City of London offered £500 for information, but neither of these produced any tangible results.

ABOVE At least two of Jack the Ripper's victims were forced on to the streets in a desperate attempt to raise the money for their lodgings.

BELOW One of the problems the police faced was that the area was very heavily populated.

The fact is that with the resources available to them at the time, and without any clues that might lead them to the killer, there was not a great deal the police could do other than increase the number of uniformed and plain-clothes officers in the district and hope that they might either glean a vital clue or be on hand to catch the killer the next time he murdered. But since that never happened, Jack the Ripper evaded capture.

In any reply to this Letter the following
Number should be quoted.

A 49354

Pressing.

WHITEHALL.

13ᵗʰ September 1888.

Sir,

I am directed by the
Secretary of State to acknowledge the
receipt of your letter of the 10ᵗʰ instant
forwarding copy of a letter from
Mr S. Montagu M.P., in which he
offers to pay a Reward of £ 100 for
the discovery and conviction of the
murderer or murderers of a woman
in Hanbury Street on the 8ᵗʰ instant,
and asking for the Secretary of States
instructions, and in reply I am to
say that, had the case been considered
a proper one for the offer of a reward

the

The Commissioner
of Metropolitan Police.

ABOVE AND OPPOSITE The government rejected any suggestion –
in this case by the police – that a reward should be offered
for information.

the Secretary of State would at once have offered one on behalf of the Government; but that the practice of offering rewards was discontinued some years ago because experience showed that in their general effect such offers produce more harm than good, and the Secretary of State thinks the present case one in which there is special risk that the offer of a reward might hinder rather than promote the ends of justice.

I am to add that the offer of a reward while any person is under arrest on suspicion is open to special objections and has not at any time been allowed.

I am, Sir,
Your obedient Servant,

E. Leigh Pemberton

286

October 1888
Philadelphia

Honorable Sir!

I take great pleasure in giving you my present whereabouts for the benefit of the Scotland Yard Boys. I am very sorry that I did not have time to finish my work with the London Whores and regret to state that I must leave them alone for a short while I am now safe in New York and will travel over to Philadelphia and when I learn the lay of the locality I might take a notion to do a little ripping there. Good bye, dear friend" I will let you hear from me before long with a little more Cutting and Ripping I said So and I fancy I will make it 48 on account of the slight delay in operations

Yours lovingly
"Jack"
the ripper

ABOVE Jack the Ripper correspondence was received from all quarters, including this letter from Philadelphia.

OPPOSITE Desperate to catch the killer, the police put out handbills asking for information.

POLICE NOTICE.

TO THE OCCUPIER.

On the mornings of Friday, 31st August, Saturday 8th, and Sunday, 30th September, 1888, Women were murdered in or near Whitechapel, supposed by some one residing in the immediate neighbourhood. Should you know of any person to whom suspicion is attached, you are earnestly requested to communicate at once with the nearest Police Station.

Metropolitan Police Office,
    30th September, 1888.

Printed by McCorquodale & Co. Limited, " The Armoury," Southwark.

THE PRESS AND THE RIPPER

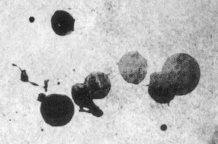

The Jack the Ripper murders generated a huge amount of press coverage. At the height of the panic, journalists from all over the world converged on the East End to report on the murders, as well as on the social conditions that they found there.

It quickly became apparent to editors that these crimes sold newspapers, since the public possessed an insatiable appetite for every salacious detail. To some, the police's seeming inability to catch the killer presented the perfect opportunity to settle old scores. To others, the crimes created a means of exposing the plight of the East End's poor to the public at large. Still more even found in themselves the opportunity to test their powers of invention.

The Metropolitan Police were suspicious of newspaper exposure and became very guarded about giving out information. Their belief was that press coverage might prove detrimental to lines of inquiry, or worse still, would alert suspects to the fact that

ABOVE W.T. Stead, the father of investigative journalism.

they were on to them. The press reacted to this lack of co-operation by finding ever more devious ways of ferreting out leads. Journalists would shadow detectives in the hope of securing that elusive scoop. They would attempt to bribe individual constables, or loosen their tongues with drink. Some even wandered round dressed as prostitutes hoping to be approached by the killer! Of course, cheque-book journalism in an area blighted by poverty could yield results. But those results might prove a double-edged sword, as people frequently told journalists what they thought they wanted to hear, or exaggerated their roles to maximize their time in the spotlight. If all else failed, the one sure way for a journalist to ensure that a story met a deadline was either to rely on local gossip or to simply make something up. Indeed, several of the fallacies, misconceptions and inaccuracies about the Ripper murders which appeared in the press in the aftermath of the killings have been repeated time and time again in subsequent books.

LEFT Newspaper sellers in London helped spread news of the Ripper murders to the populace at large.

Some newspapers were appalled by the sensationalism of their competitors and worried about the effects it was having. The *Star*'s campaign to alert the public to the menace of "Leather Apron" is illustrative of this. The *Daily News* was quick to point out that: "The public are looking for a monster, and in the legend of "Leather Apron" the Whitechapel part of them seem to be inventing a monster to look for. This kind of invention ought to be discouraged in every possible way, or there may soon be murders from panic to add to murders from lust of blood …"

Responsible reporting aside, had it not been for a journalist's powers of invention there is a good chance that the Jack the Ripper murders would not have achieved their posthumous notoriety. When the police released the "Dear Boss" letter, its chilling moniker was seized upon by the press at large as the perfect name to convey to their readers the horror of what was happening in Whitechapel.

As the journalist George Sims observed "… JACK THE RIPPER is the hero of the hour. A gruesome wag, a grim practical joker, has succeeded in getting an enormous amount of fun out of a postcard which he sent to the Central News. The fun is all his own, and nobody shares in it, but he must be gloating demonically at the present moment at the state of perturbation in which he has flung the public mind …"

The police themselves were convinced almost from the outset that the letter was a hoax and that it had, in fact, been written by a journalist, and several officers even claimed to know who he was.

His identity today is of little consequence. What is of consequence is his legacy. For, whoever he might have been, that journalist created a name which elevated a homicidal East End nobody into the realm of legend.

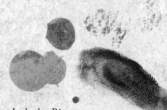

LEFT The name Jack the Ripper originally came from a letter sent to a London news agency.

WHITECHAPEL, 1888.

Member of "Criminal Class." "Fine Body o' Men, the Per-leece!"

Ditto. "Uncommon Fine!—It's Lucky for Hus as There's Sech a Bloomin' Few on 'em!!!"

"I have to observe that the Metropolitan Police have not large reserves doing nothing and ready to meet emergencies; but every man has his duty allotted to him, and I can only strengthen the Whitechapel district by drawing men from duty in other parts of the Metropolis."—*Sir Charles Warren's Letter.* "There is one Policeman to every seven hundred persons."—*Vide Recent Statistics.*

ABOVE AND OPPOSITE Press images such as these helped foster public opinion of both the police and the murders.

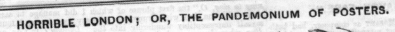

HORRIBLE LONDON; OR, THE PANDEMONIUM OF POSTERS.

A space in a slum, or a blank
   on a fence,
A spare square of brick in a
   neighbourhood dense,
   Or a bit of unoccupied
     boarding,
But there the new poster, who
   didn't much care
For the menacing legend,
   " Bill-stickers beware ! "
   Right soon was tremen-
     dously busy
With placards portentous in
   purple and blue,   [hue,
Of horrible subject and hideous
Enough to bemuddle an aëro-
   naut's view,
   And turn the best steeple-
     Jack dizzy.
Oh, the flamboyant flare of
   those fiendish designs,
With their sanguine paint-
   splashes and sinister lines!
   Gehenna seemed visibly
     glaring
In paint from those villanous
   daubs.   There were men
At murderous work in mal-
   odorous den,
   And ghoul-woman grue-
     somely staring.
The whole sordid drama of
   murder and guilt,
The steel that strikes home, and
   the blood that is spilt,
   Was pictured in realist
     colours,
With emphasis strong on the
   black and the red,
The fear of the stricken, the
   glare of the dead ;
   All dreads and disasters and
     dolours
That haunt poor Humanity's
   dismallest state,
The horrors of crime and the
   terrors of fate,
   As conceived by the crudest
     of fancies,
Were limned on these posters
   in terrible tints,
In the style of the vilest sen-
   sational prints
   Or the vulgarest penny
     romances.

That Bill-sticker paused in his
   work with a look
Which betrayed the black de-
   mon, and gleesomely shook
   His sides in a spasm of
     laughter.
Quoth he, with a sinister wag
   of his head,
" By my horns, the good artist
   has lavished the red !
This home of coarse horror—
   this house of the dead
   Looks crimson from base-
     ment to rafter.
How strange that a civilised
   City—ho! ho!
'Tis their fatuous dream to
   consider it so !—
   Which is nothing too lovely at
     best, should bestow
Such a liberal licence on
   spoilers !
These mural monstrosities,
   reeking of crime,
Flaring horridly forth amidst
   squalor and grime,
   Must have an effect which will
     tell in good time
Upon legions of dull-witted
   toilers.

THE Demon set forth in a novel disguise
(All methods of mischief the master-fiend tries)
Quoth he, " There's much ill to be wrought through
   the eyes.
   I think, without being a boaster,
I can give their most 'cute Advertisers a start,
And beat them all round at the Bill-sticker's art.
I will set up in business in Babylon's mart,
   As the new Pandemonium Poster ! "
So he roved the huge city with wallet at waist,
With a brush, and a stick, and a pot full of paste,
   And there wasn't a wall or a hoarding,

THE NEW YORK HERALD.

NO. 222.   LONDON EDITION, WEDNESDAY, SEPTEMBER 11, 1889.   PRICE ONE PENNY.

DOES HE KNOW THE RIPPER?

WHO IS THIS MAN THAT CALLED AT THE "HERALD" OFFICE SUNDAY.

He was Positive a Murder Had Been Committed at Twenty Minutes Past Eleven o'clock on Saturday Night, on the Spot Where the Dead and Mutilated Body of a Woman was Found Yesterday—Mystery of Mysteries.

London in general, and Whitechapel in particular, were thrown into a feverish state of excitement yesterday morning by the news that "Jack the Ripper" had murdered and mutilated his ninth victim. Both the murder and the mutilation were reported to be, and indeed proved to be, more horrible than in any one of the eight cases preceding. The quick and close review of the facts by the police department led to the conclusion late yesterday afternoon that the remains did not represent "Jack the Ripper's" handiwork, and this may or may not be true.

There is a very extraordinary feature, however, in this case, which has been lacking in all the others. That it is extraordinary no one will doubt who reads the brief story of last Saturday night as detailed below. If the woman found in the archway was a victim of "Jack the Ripper," it is positively sure either that the murderer has been seen by many people, or that another man who knew of the murder and all the circumstances so long ago as last Saturday

POLICE CONSTABLE PENNETT, WHO FOUND THE BODY.

night is abroad, and can be found, if the police are clever enough. On the other hand, last Saturday night's events indicate to some extent that the body found yesterday, be it that of a murdered woman or a body from a dissecting room, was in the hands of more than one man who knew all about it, because on last Saturday night a man betrayed the whole affair. The circumstances are as follows, and will be verified in every particular by evidence, should the police or department desire.

Last Sunday morning, at five minutes past nine o'clock, a young man called at the HERALD office and inquired that there was another "Jack the Ripper" murder. He was sent up to the editorial rooms and interviewed by the night editor. He said that a mutilated body had been found in Backchurch-lane, in Whitechapel. He said that it had been found by a policeman at twenty minutes past eleven o'clock. The map of London was immediately studied by two reporters in order to locate Backchurch-lane, while the editor cross-questioned the man. He said it had been told to him by an acquaintance of his, a police inspector whom he had met in Backchurch High-street. He said there was no doubt about it, and that he had hurried to the HERALD office understanding that he would be rewarded for the news. He said his name was John Cleary, and that he lived at 21, White Horse-yard, Drury-lane. He was asked to write down his name and address, and did so, the writing being preserved. His information was explicit and seemingly authentic, and two reporters were detailed to take the man with them, and go and get the story.

The two reporters went out, and one of them stopped on the stairway of the stairway in going down, and asked the man some more questions. Under this examination he varied slightly, saying that the man who had told him was not a police inspector, but an ex-member of the police force. This statement has, perhaps, some significance too all who have been following the murders closely. He then went down to the street with the reporters. They called a hansom and told the man to get in with them; but he first hesitated, and then refused. His excuse was that it was too far from his home. They urged him to go, but he was firm. One of them proposed to take him back upstairs, in order to have him near at hand if necessary; but the necessity of immediate departure compelled them to start and leave the man to go his own way. He was assured that if the news proved authentic he would be handsomely rewarded, and he went away apparently contented with the arrangement.

The two reporters drove rapidly to Backchurch-lane, and found it without difficulty. They made a thorough search of the neighborhood. They went down so far as the archway where the body was found yesterday morning, but found all quiet and no trace of any murder. They met two police officers, one an inspector and the other a

constable. They questioned both, and told them the report they had heard, and these two officers can verify the enquiry. They all heard nothing, and reported. In fact, it is certainly true that on Sunday morning a murdered and mutilated body was reported as having been found in Backchurch-lane, and that exactly such a body was found there yesterday morning.

The matter was passed over as unimportant on Sunday and Monday. The moment that the body was found yesterday, however, the events of Sunday morning loomed up with a significance rather colossal, and a hunt began for John Cleary.

SIDE VIEW OF THE ARCH WHERE THE BODY WAS FOUND.

of 21, White Horse-yard, Drury-lane. Mr. John Cleary, however, was not known at No. 21, or anywhere else in White Horse-yard, Drury-lane. The house is a four-story one. The street floor is vacant, the first and second floors are occupied by families, and the top floor by a widow woman with two children. The widow woman was confident that no young man by the name of John Cleary either lived in the house or had ever lived there. The people in every house in White Horse-yard were questioned under circumstances which deposed them to tell all they knew, but nobody had ever heard the name of John Cleary, and everybody said that no man of that name could have lived there without their knowing it, which was quite true. It became evident, therefore, that the man had given a false address, and in all probability a false name, as a precaution in the matter of residence would scarcely have been taken, and the precaution as to name neglected.

"Cleary's" description, however, had been carefully taken. He was a young man, apparently between twenty-five and twenty-eight years of age. He was short, his height being about 5ft. 4in. He was of medium build, and weighed about 160lb. He was light-complexioned, had a small fair moustache and blue eyes. On his left cheek was an inflamed spot, which looked as of a boil had lately been there and was healing. He wore a dark coat and waistcoat. His shirt was not seen, the space at the throat being covered by a dirty white handkerchief tied about his neck. His trousers were dark velveteen, so soiled at the knees as to indicate that he blacked shoes. He had worn a round, black, soft felt. He walked with a shuffle and spoke in the usual fashion of the developing citizen of Whitechapel, whom, in all respects, he resembled.

It is thus certain that there was an intention on the part of the party or parties who had the body in keeping to place it in Backchurch-lane Saturday night, where it was found yesterday. If coincidences be of any value, it may be noted that this was the anniversary of the Hanbury-street murder. It is beyond doubt that "Cleary" got wind of the scheme, if he was not one of the principals. That the original intention was that carried out would indicate that he was an outsider acquainted with the project, who hoped to profit by it. There seems to be no reason to doubt that the body was not found by the police until yesterday morning, and that it was placed there about that time before scenes reasonably sure. Nevertheless, "John Cleary," whoever he may be, must know all about the mystery, and is certainly the most valuable man in the pursuit of the police at the present time.

The mutilated body of "Jack the Ripper's" latest victim, if such it is, was discovered about half-past five o'clock yesterday morning beneath a railway arch on the south side of Pinchin-street, which runs eastward from Backchurch-lane

FULL VIEW OF THE ARCH WHERE THE BODY WAS FOUND.

narrow thoroughfare connecting Commercial-road with Cable-street. The locality is about half a mile southward from the busiest district which has been the centre of "the Ripper's" murders. It is, however, no more distant than was the Buck's-row crime, which was the third, and the point is less than three minutes from the scene of the fifth murder, the one in Berner-street. It is about the same distance from the Leman-street police-station. The south side of Pinchin-street is skirted by a long series of high brick arches, supporting the roadway of the London, Tilbury, and Great Eastern Railway. The arch beneath which the body was found is the only one which is open, the others being boarded up, or filled with loose doors, and used for storage and like purposes. This particular arch had been boarded up, as the joists stretching across it indicated, but the boards had been torn off and carried away for firewood by the people in the vicinity, a policeman said. Anyone passing along Pinchin-street can easily see within three arches. Both officer Pennett and another patrolman say that they passed by the spot between half past four and five o'clock, and saw nothing out of the common.

The discovery was made by Officer Pennett at half-past five o'clock. In passing along his beat, he flashed his bull's-eye into the dark arch and noticed a bundle which excited his curiosity, as it but not been three half an hour before. He went in and inspected it and was startled to find it the trunk of a naked woman.

The remains were lying face downward. The head and legs had been removed, and the right was so grotesque and horrible that the constable was some seconds in making out what it really was. The horrible mass was partly covered by a blood-stained chemise, much disarranged. Officer Pennett immediately whistled for assistance, and was quickly joined by several patrolmen. Word was sent to headquarters, and in a short time a group of inspectors and officials stood around the remains. When examined it appeared that the head and legs had been very neatly dissevered, and a search of the whole vicinity revealed no trace of them. There was one long cut down the centre of the body. The remains, so far as could be told by the examination, were those of a woman between thirty-two and forty years of age, rather short and of a dark complexion. It was evident from the doctor's examination that she had never had a child.

SCENE OF THE WHITECHAPEL MURDERS.

NAMES OF VICTIMS AND DATES OF THE CRIMES.

1. An unknown woman, Christmas week, 1887.
2. Martha Turner, found stabbed in 39 places on landing at George-yard buildings, Commercial street, Spitalfields, August 7, 1888.
3. Mrs. Mary Ann Nichols, in Buck's-row, August 31, 1888.
4. Mrs. Annie Chapman, Hanbury-street, Sept. 7, 1888.

5. Elizabeth Stride, Berner-street, Sept. 30, 1888.
6. Catherine Eddowes, Mitre-square, Sept. 30, 1888.
7. Mary Jane Kelly, 26, Dorset-street, Spitalfields.
8. Alice Mackenzie, July 17, 1889.
9. Body of unknown woman found in Backchurch-lane, Cable-street, Sept. 10.

There was a mark about the waist such as would have been left by an excessive rope. There was no clothing about the chemise, which was an ordinary cotton one. There was no blood upon the ground, and all the bloodstains were dry, showing that the murder, if it had been a murder, had taken place some days before. It was evident that the body had been located three in the condition in which it had been found. There is ample evidence that it was brought there at some time during the night. From the way in which it lay, it appeared to have been hurriedly dropped there and to have been untouched afterwards by the person who brought it. The body was discovered in several places, and decomposition was setting in at the edge of the

ENTRANCE TO ST. GEORGE'S BUILDINGS.

cuts. Everything indicated that death had taken place four or five days previously.

The remains were removed to St. George's mortuary, and were there viewed by a HERALD reporter. The body, lying on the slab in the centre of the mean little room, was a piteous and revolting spectacle. The severance of the head and legs seemed to have taken from it the fashion of humanity, and it needed a second glance to recognize the true character of the mass of inert flesh. The body stripped to be that

of a young and well-formed woman, well nourished and perfectly healthy. Except the mutilations already spoken of the only marks of violence it bore were the dark blue traces of finger marks about and below the elbow of the left arm and a shapeless bruise on the right wrist. The singularity of the mutilations was that the cuts

DUCK'S ROW, GREAT EASTERN SQUARE.

were made with perfect cleanness and decision. There was no mangling of the flesh. The operation had been performed as neatly as if it had been done by a practical surgeon in the quiet of a dissecting room, rather than by a brutal miscreant in the confusion and terror of committing a hideous crime. A singular circumstance, it is inconceivable with the marks of putrefaction on other parts of the body, borne out also by the stench of decay, is that the flesh of the stump of the right thigh was bright and red as with a recent effusion of blood. The flesh of the other stump and of the neck was dry and caked, as were the lips of the gaping cut extending from the breastbone to the root of the thigh, exposing the intestines, which, however, have been left intact, contrary to the practice of the Whitechapel butcher, to whom so many attribute this crime. The decapitation and the cutting off of the limbs are also opposed to his practice, and help in great doubt on that theory, and to suggest that the crime much more nearly resembles those recently committed at Rainham and Battersea. Beside the body lay the torn and bloodstained rags of the chemise, which had been lying over the body, the only scrap of material, except the body itself, yet found which which may possibly assist the police in the task of identification.

THE HUNT FOR CLUES.

Scotland Yard was vastly astir. Before six o'clock a message was received there from Leman-street. It was only "Whitechapel again," but it suffered to put things instantly into a ferment. Word was at once sent to Commissioner Monro and the Assistant Commissioners, and they immediately responded. Two fresh detectives were placed on the case "Inspector Abberline, who has been following it, being out of town. The hunt for clues and fore determination began vigorously. The first list of evidence was a blood-stained entanglement found at half-past seven in a vacant yard in Hooper-street, 500 yards in the fence, and it was turned over to the police. The chains on this, as on the chemise, were old and dried. This came the story of a man who said he had seen another man with a heavy bundle of something on his back, about four o'clock. He was questioned, but his information was not important, the police feeling confident that the body was brought nearly to the spot in a vehicle of some kind. Chief Commissioner Monro and Colonel Monsell,

COURT WHERE BODY WAS FOUND IN HANBURY STREET.

Chief Constable, went all over the ground, and visited the mortuary. Three arrests were made in the shape of two sailors and a shoeblack found sleeping in an adjacent archway, but after being examined at the Leman-street Station they were released, it being evident that they knew nothing of the matter. It shortly appeared that there was no more of a clue in the case than there had been in the preceding ones. Mr. Williamson, of the Criminal Investigation department, admitted that when questioned as to whether the police had as yet formed any theory regarding the case. He replied:—"There is not evidence enough yet on which to base any theory. As a matter of fact, the police are not so found of rushing into theorizing as some of you gentlemen of the Press seem to think. One fact is worth half a dozen theories, and in this case we have to bend our energies to the discovery of facts. This one promises to be one of peculiar difficulty. The others were mysterious enough, but here the mystery is complete; the head being gone, the chances of identification are very slight. People who are inclined to be impatient with the police should remember how enormous the difficulties of such a case as this are. Do I think it is "Jack the Ripper" again? As I said, I have no theories. I wait for facts."

The remains lay all day at the Morgue, but were not identified. Identification will, in fact, be difficult, if not impossible. The only assisting fact was one revealed by Secretary Bartlett to a HERALD reporter at the Old Jewry in the afternoon. He said that a week ago a woman's hand had been picked up in Shoreditch, and all efforts to trace its owner and origin had thus far failed.

The River Police were put on the alert within twenty minutes after the finding of the body. The despatch sent to them and to all the other Metropolitan stations was as follows:—

At twenty minutes to six was found of a woman found under the arches in Pinchin-street. Age about forty. Height 5ft. 3in. Hair dark brown. No clothing except the chemise, very much torn and blood stained. Both elbows discolored, as if from habitual leaning on them. Post-mortem. Marks around waist, apparently caused by a rope.

Immediately upon the circulation of this telegram, the Thames Police, under Detective-Inspector Regan and Chief-inspector Moore, assisted by Sergeants Moore, Francis, Howard, Davis, and Scott, at once got their various craft on the river, and boarded all the vessels at the mouth of the Thames and in the docks. Attention was particularly directed to the cattle boats and those from Spain and America. Among those boarded in the London Docks were the City of the Cadiz, the Malaga, and the Gallicia, and the Lydian Monarch in the Millwall Docks. The operation of searching these vessels had not concluded until a late hour in the evening, and so far as the investigation had gone the captains of the various vessels were able to give satisfactory accounts as to their crews.

After the removal of the remains to the mortuary, Mr. Clarke, Dr. Gordon Brown (the chief police-surgeon), and two other medical gentlemen who had experience in previous cases of this nature, shortly after made a more careful examination of the remains. It was noticed that the trunk displayed green patches; the flesh otherwise was white. The doctors, from their investigations, concluded that the cuts had been inflicted not clearly from the loin, showing no signs of a separating instrument. Nothing whatever was found to be missing except those members and the head. The cut severing the head from the body was skilfully done, there being no hacking or clumsy dissection noticeable. Furthermore, a saw had been used to sever the bones in such a way as to leave no doubt that the person responsible for the dismemberment possessed a good knowledge of anatomy. There were no signs about the hands which would indicate that the woman had been used to hard work, and so far as could be seen there had been no attempt to obliterate or mark on one of the fingers, apparently caused by a ring.

SCENE OF THE MITRE SQUARE CRIME.

commenced on the left side and carried to the right with a clean sweep. The same peculiarity was observed in the other wounds, and in separating the legs more flesh had been cut from the trunk on the left side than on the other. In more than one of the previous crimes this peculiarity has been observed and commented upon. The legs are taken out cleanly from the loin, showing no signs of a separating instrument. Nothing whatever was found to be missing except those members and the head.

The body was well nourished and cared for. One of the several doctors who viewed the remains expressed the opinion that had he been asked to dissect the body in the manner in which he saw it he could not have done it more neatly and skilfully. In consequence of the similarity in the mode of dismemberment pursued in this case and those of the recent Battersea and Rainham mysteries, the officers engaged in those cases were consulted, and their general opinion is that the resemblances in all cases are so remarkable as to give grounds for the belief that the present crime is one with a different origin to that of the previous Whitechapel atrocities.

DOCTORS AND POLICE CONSULT.

A conference to which it is believed considerable importance is attached took place last evening at the Leman-street Police-station. When Dr. Phillips was telegraphed for to Bournemouth he replied that he would return to town at once; but

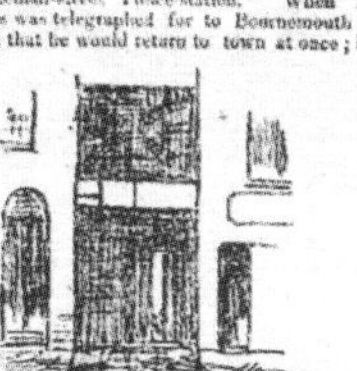

ENTRANCE TO BERNER STREET COURT.

asked the authorities to adjourn the post-mortem in the meantime. He arrived in London about five p.m. last evening, and after making some preliminary investigations attended at Leman-street Police-station soon after six o'clock. He was closeted with the Chief Constable Colonel Monsell, Mr. Arnold, and the officers from Scotland Yard. At seven p.m. Mr. Monro, the Chief Commissioner, arrived at the station in his private carriage, and joined in the deliberation, which continued until nearly nine o'clock.

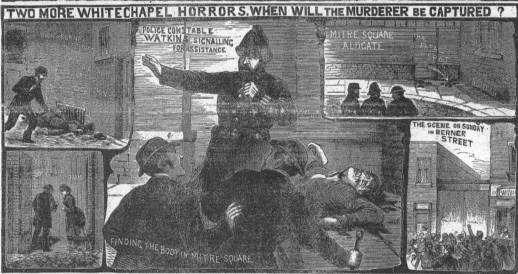

THE FIFTH VICTIM of the WHITECHAPEL FIEND.

FINDING the MUTILATED BODY IN MITRE SQARE

OPPOSITE The *New York Herald* was just one of the international newspapers that reported on the killings.

ABOVE The *Illustrated Police News* treated its readers to lurid depictions of the crimes; whether these were primarily for information or ghoulish curiosity is unclear.

JACK THE RIPPER'S LONDON TODAY

At first glance it might appear that little, if anything, of Jack the Ripper's London has survived. Whereas this is most certainly true with regard the actual murder sites, all of which have now been obliterated, there are still sections of the East End that have changed little since 1888.

Buck's Row, where Mary Nichols died on 31 August 1888, disappeared, in name at least, shortly after her death. The local residents became ashamed of their sudden notoriety, and successfully petitioned the council to change its name to Durward Street. A small, litter-strewn car park now stands on the murder site itself. One building, however, has survived in the immediate vicinity. The looming bulk of the Board School towers over the street, just as it did in 1888, although today it has been converted into flats.

A short distance away, the London Hospital still stands on Whitechapel High Street. It was here that Emma Smith, the first Whitechapel Murders victim, died, and here worked Dr Openshaw, whose opinion was sought in connection with the piece of kidney that George Lusk had received, along with his letter "From Hell".

Closer to the City of London, and also on Whitechapel High Street, the White Hart pub, in the cellar of which suspect George Chapman worked as a barber in 1890, still dispenses frothing tankards of ale to

thirsty Ripper enthusiasts. Adjoining it is the sinister arch through which Martha Tabram took her soldier client in the early hours of 7 August 1888. It leads into the cobble-stoned Gunthorpe Street, where her body was discovered in George Yard, and which, at night, can be just as sinister

and threatening as it was in 1888.

Round the corner on Brick Lane, the Sheraz Curry Restaurant now occupies the building that was the Frying Pan pub. Here Mary Nichols drank away her doss money on the night of her murder. Close scrutiny of its upper storeys reveals that two crossed frying pans still adorn its upper gable, along with its original name "Ye Frying Pan".

A rather ugly brewery building stands on the site of 29 Hanbury Street, in the back yard of which the body of Annie Chapman was found at 6 a.m. on 8 September 1888. The opposite section of Hanbury Street, the south side, is more or less intact, so it is possible at least to gain an impression of what the north side would have looked like at the time of the murder.

Nearby, on the busy Commercial Street, the Ten Bells pub, linked with the final hours of both Annie Chapman and Mary Kelly, is still doing a roaring trade, although it has made a concerted effort to distance itself from its Ripper-related past.

Opposite it stands one of the neighbourhood's most poignant buildings, the soaring white tower of Christchurch, Spitalfields. It dominates its surroundings today, just as it did in 1888, a towering and breathtaking edifice at which Jack the Ripper's victims might well have glanced

OPPOSITE The arched entrance into George Yard (now Gunthorpe Street) is still as sinister as it must have been then.

LEFT Every one of Jack the Ripper's victims would have gazed up at this church, Christchurch, Spitalfields, on an almost daily basis.

on an almost daily basis.

Of Berner Street, where Elizabeth Stride was killed on 30 September, nothing has survived. The site itself is now occupied by a school playground. Likewise, Mitre Square, where Catherine Eddowes became the Ripper's next victim that same morning, has seen its old warehouse buildings replaced by a school and nondescript office buildings.

One building, however, does survive from the night of the double murder. Less than 10 minutes' walk away, Wentworth Model Dwellings rise over Goulston Street, and the doorway where the bloodstained piece of Catherine's apron was found is now the take-away counter of the Happy Days Fish and Chip Shop.

Back on Commercial Street and across the road from Christchurch, a car park now occupies the site of Dorset Street, where Mary Kelly was murdered on 9 November 1888. A food warehouse now stands over the site of Miller's Court, where her body was found. But the former Providence Row night shelter still looms over Dorset Street's west end. It is the only building in the immediate vicinity that connects to that long- ago night when a lone cry of "murder" spelt the end of Jack the Ripper's reign of terror.

IN LOVING MEMORY OF
MARIE JEANETTE KELLY
NONE BUT THE LONELY HEARTS
CAN KNOW MY SADNESS
LOVE LIVES FOREVER.

OPPOSITE The Ten Bells pub on Commercial Street, still serving the local area as it did in 1888.

ABOVE People still lay flowers on the grave of Mary Kelly at St Patrick's Roman Catholic Cemetery, Leyton.

BELOW Catherine Eddowes is remembered by a plaque in the City of London Cemetery.

CITY OF LONDON CEMETERY

Catherine Eddowes

Died 30th September 1888

HERITAGE TRAIL

WORST BRITON EVER

In January 2006, Jack the Ripper topped a poll held by *BBC History Magazine* to find the worst Briton ever. The magazine's editor, David Musgrove, observed that, "The public's choice … reflects the fact that the Victorian murderer remains an iconic figure today, and perhaps is seen by many as the forerunner of the serial killers that society has had to deal with since the Ripper's time." Professor Clive Emsley, of the Open University, and the man who originally nominated the Ripper, added, "The Ripper has become a villain – for all time – and his shadow extends to the present day."

INDEX

Page numbers in *italic type* refer to pictures or their captions.

CREDITS